Ground Water

Ground Water

Colin Browne

Talonbooks
2002

Talonbooks
P.O. Box 2076, Vancouver, British Columbia, Canada V6B 3S3
www.talonbooks.com

Typeset in Adobe Caslon and printed and bound in Canada.

First Printing: June 2002

National Library of Canada Cataloguing in Publication Data

Browne, Colin, 1946-
  Ground water

Poems.
  ISBN 0-88922-465-X

  I. Title.
PS8553.R69G76 2002   C811'.54   C2002-910065-8
PR9199.3.B717G76 2002

The publisher gratefully acknowledges the financial support of the Canada
Council for the Arts; the Government of Canada through the Book Publishing
Industry Development Program; and the Province of British Columbia through
the British Columbia Arts Council for our publishing activities.

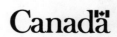

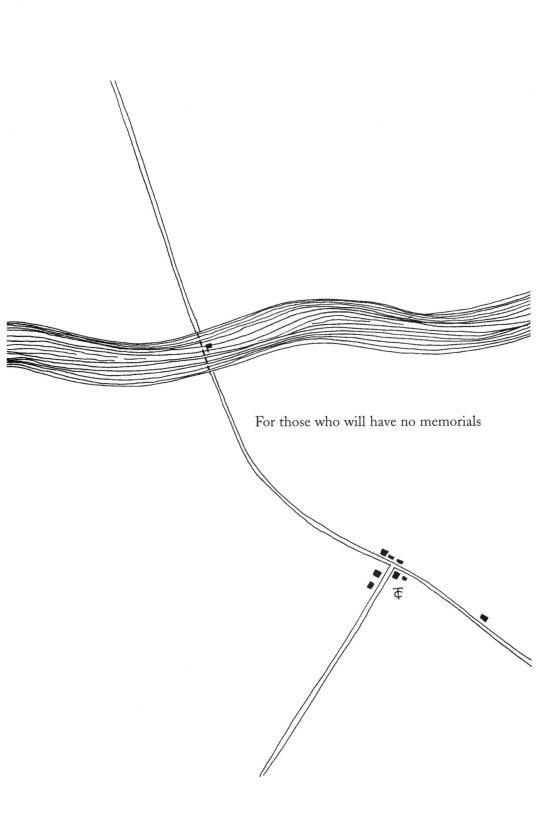

For those who will have no memorials

Better get used to yourself.

Susanna Browne (aged 3 1/2)
climbing the gangplank at low tide
on the Maple Bay government wharf

a
line
leaves

(m)leans
b(l)inds

prep/prop

fallen bull
hair pin

a *picture* of
an idea

a   idea

inscribed, or
inscribing itself

or its
shadow

if
shadow

of what
longing
b?

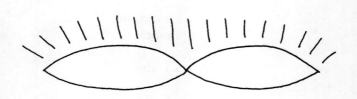

Ground Water

A Performance for Music and Text

Music by Martin Gotfrit
Text by Colin Browne

I (Maul)

0.   A rip. A limb. The hole you fell through. The tunnel you tore. The hole you harrowed. The breach you bear. The shaft you flourish. The river we bank on. Thicket. Hatchet. Bundle of twigs. A gullet; the puncture.

1.   "We walked down to the Point that first evening. There was an open mossy place. I sat, content. He insisted on a dark sort of crevice, all dank and wet with shreds of seaweed hanging off sticks."

2.   It fits your hand. Glans. Jammed pleasure tube. It fits your hand. Its shaft. Tip. "The trees went forth *on a time* to anoint a king over them...." Longing for it, an irreducible before— Wessex as brake, or the glade Virgilian—time as place as bung: "*locus ille locorum.*" The berried hedges of Arcadia mia. Prophylaxis, pop. What penetrates. "...golden dishes...golden cups." "Rivers at their feet." Currency. Paternity. Auguries of redistribution. Bramble led them, bramble bled them. Okay. "*Dicite, quandoquidem in molli consedimus herba.*" How are you (we) all out there (here) in Paradise?

3.   Do you remember the cut above Narbonne? Link men, silk. Silk. Grass like silk. Spun grass. Cuffs. Rock breach. Stars. The little Republican light bulbs of Figueras. "*...y aparacen las sendas / impenetrables*"—look!

4.   Hard put. Hand job. Hard harp, gripped. Harm jar. Hunh! Stalk. Stem. Gripped harp. Hunh! Tip. Cut. Pitted. Maul. It fits your hand. Hunh! Glans. Haft. Jammed pleasure tube. It fits your hand. Hand-shaped. Heart-shaped. Haven-shaped. Hunh! Jarama-shaped. Ebro-shaped. Turia-shaped. Manzanares-shaped. Hunh!

5.   Oh, the narcissi! As if a "view" "induced" or were selectively osmotic. Arboreal chrome. Branches of husbandry or tinkering for crow's feet the cosmetic measure of an equestrian paradiddle through appropriated landscapes. Take *this* splendid Second Edition "*locus amoenus*", scarcely a mile from the Brentwood Texaco and up past the Reserve on your left. Transposable gates, gloom. Fig. Primrose. Honeysuckle. Broom. A speckle of feldspar. Hedge, a bower. Mantled dominion.

6.   "*Amnis ibat inter herbas valle fusus frigida....*" Approximate botanical cenotaphs or rude monikers fixed *parouisa* in memory as strategically-mown lawn. "For I would only ask thereof / That thy worm should be my worm, Love." Archimedian logistics. His grave loomed, wrist-like, in the colonial surd.

7.   They proceeded along a wooded path, single file. She smelled something, the honey dripping out of arbutus flowers. "Smell," she said, "*this* is paradise."

8.   It was always a version of somewhere else. Kerbs. Scales. A paucity of gristle. Notion of retreat at bottom. My sweet, tiny, child, all this, all this....

9.   Hoots. Clamps. Boys as burning tires clutching their bellies. Wild roses. "Bomb craters visible on the streets, simply fabulous...." A poker to roll them over with. Affordable rapture in the limbs of immigrant men. A leer. The page after the last page she ran into. Dazzle on the water. Here on this platform they were or wore their Sunday best. The fruit that month profited him significantly. Fees docked in a higher order's service proved persuasive. Retribution. Perfectibility. The golden wounds of their children running in the street. The

dream announcer called our names saying, "This is Lee Carter the Saanichton Sweetheart with the Starlighters Orchestra and one of last year's biggest successes…."

Song: "*Don't sit under the apple tree with anyone else but me…*"

10.   Orphée, Orphée, in your Chevrolet,
come in, come in, come in.

II (Steamer)

1.   Heartland. The smell of it. He said I'm leaving now and a few things. A green car, straw, an old Volkswagen's flare. These pungent trunks—split, arced. Light cleaving to twigs, molten among buds—"*Nunc frondent silvae, nunc formosissimus annus....*" She'd knelt to sniff an estimated noise of violets. "Where is your forgiveness?" she inquired. In the gutter, page 5, he glossed "Laws", then rubbed it out, then, "Natural Law & Economic Law." A crimp. A trough. The customary ampersand. Snow falling; those trees grew dark and warm.

2.   "I thought it the fairest land I had ever set eyes on. The valley was prairie like with large oak trees scattered over it, covered with grass among which the blue camas and yellow buttercups were scattered and there was a knoll near covered with wild strawberries." The symmetry!

3.   "*Sint in eo diversae arbores et fructus in eis dependentes....*" An infestation, red mites. Seething in the grasses and a whiff of rain. Pear boughs heaped in fasces at each trunk's penetration. Standing in him and him. "...providing employment...leisure...what it is you want...goods and services to provide a high standard of living...." Thicket. Hatchet. Almost beside himself. At night invisible sea animals blazed on her skin. *Amoenitatis locus*. Thicket of flowering damson. "...what it is you are trying to do—what end...." One morning there I discovered a rat tipped worshipfully into my sheets. "...money...wealth and goods and services...unpurchasable production...." Arbutus at dusk affirmed tentative semblance to something else, sheep or fish, deer perhaps. A deflective discourse. *Amoenitatis locus*—heartland—"loveliest of places." Pruning to stimulate union. The smell when burned. He was hunting for something from a book, call it buried terraces, back-up memory or "worried by the dogs." Wort veer. Walls buttercup cleaves. Fibres swollen, irritant vapour. Juniper.

Yew. Flicker's play on blue dependers. She held his hand and his hand went milky. It made the hairs stand up on her swim. "...redundant machinery...mills and factories...farms and fields...symptoms...common disease...lack of purchasing power...specific of which money has to be made...." The exotics he was sticking in. "We walked down to the point. Six men in two canoes came by, hunting ducks." This they see in Orion. Venus plummets promptly.

4.   How lovely in the morning to gaze out on discharge in the ring, saying regard the light and the light always dying: "*La gloria di colui che tutto move / per l'universo penetra*...." Look : a "real" "thing" : bamboo dowels and twine. Lid plus basket. Wind. A little broccoli. Quince, willow. That head yearning in the river.... "...*te, dulcis coniunx, te solo in litore*.... The house, the orchard, the lawns, vines clinging to vines. Enforced austerities. Ruins. Stains. Heartland. An economy of longing. It was always a version of somewhere else.

5.   Villanueva de la Canada, 1937: "Wherever you looked we saw nothing but targets and more targets." Father!

III (Teabox)

1.   Lawn trimming as an arc of memory. Recaulking as a single arc of someone never penetrating. At the back door a possible rose, a hydrangea neutralized by ritual applications. A surplus. "CREATING…assuming for the moment that we have the power to do…." Stationing the jasmine a snap, its heroic flare a natural for junctions. "…surplus productive capacity…specific of which money has to be made…monopoly of credit…." The price of metal, for instance. What counts. Anxious brows of Europe. Gravel, falling stucco. Cracks. "Nature and education" —a kind of automatic pilot. Intervention as it profits. He'd enough trouble finding cheap white labour. And always, always, acquisition's melancholy *tristesse*…. He pondered saxifrage along the north-east bed. Or the way heat collected, why not another Gravenstein? "…tangible wealth at the bank…custodian…nothing like that…." The name irked. You were made with love in our hearts and now already one is a parcel called gift we are fighting for in a distant land.

2.   Moss a Louis in his Jerusalem. Beneath the mould fungus tore a path. Spinous commodities, arched across the shack without regard for doctrine, designated the limits of observance for them all. "…two ways…drive a wedge…reflect the actual truth…three or four years…." He approached his desktop with conviction. He carried his tools into the alders. He barked. A man tore her apart in a nearby town. "Why was it everything," she wrote, "was so…easier when we had animals' heads on?"

3.   That private European in his faraway garden, in the predetermined pure valley, nights the drums assailed hims, swept hims down the hole of his own pelt's shaft. "I was no bachelor and I knew if I were to succeed I would have to have a wife, and I made up my mind not to marry an Indian woman as most of my countrymen had, as I had lived among them long

enough to make up my mind." All night that drumming, drumming. That imperial infinitive.

4. She came to visualize herself as a grape hyacinth's final fit beneath a fir. "Dear mother," she wrote, "nothing here is like a miniature anything else." Vehicles crushed the verandah. "We dubbed them days yet they seemed holes without danger." Cash stalked berries; she "lived for" scenery. So many dull hues passed for animation. She laid out objects in the cupboard, objects she'd employ directly, objects to send home for. Holes opened or closed. She adjusted her Brownie to make things take place. All night she twiddled the yellow eye....

5. There were no children only tin things in privileged notions. During the interlude he was otherwise preoccupied and sought bed as beef cooks or trimmed fork suckers. Paradise in this version indicated time investments without negotiable fears. Bundles of sticks, their little hot-dog hatchets. In our case tiny stones and pips were considered unmerchandiseable. One inserts years after the gravel stains. She gasped to see the mergansers. "Look," she said, "mergansers."

6. His anguished hacking. Fecund, too manipulable trees. Thickets. The "monopoly of credit" obsessed him. It was always aversion to somewhere else. Lost ground, lost chances. Service betrayed. His colleagues, for example, on the "the banking race". His groomed libido, his rigour, his pamphlet by *il miglior fabbro*. Their nose for caste. Heartland. A phantom limb. "…ticket…price…make up the lack…." Then the scheme with the Party on the Douglasite model. Lapel pins and rubber stamps. The little green crosses. Folding. Licking. Spermhead, his lovely vowels. The breached garden bricked in.

7.   Its top slid off. A woman pushing hard on another woman's groin. *Le paradis terrestre*…. It was always a version of somewhere else.

IV (Bread Knife)

1.   *Amo. Amas. Amat. Amamus. Amatus. Amant.*
(repeat)

2.   A mat. A matting. Needles in cakes or the worn rosemary
clings to cheese. Clumps, clings, badges of light. Flickers, moss.
That head in the river.

3.   Mould. A slug glistening in it. Glands, their modest chastity.
Worn poles. Rubber-smeared rocks, torqued. Tombs. Thickets.
Sun leaking through vine stumps. The gap. The tunnel. "We
are not afraid of ruins; we are going to inherit the earth."

4.   As simple as a child withdrew it one day to whittle. Sparkle on
liquid. The Duce awakes and his dream swims out of him. "We
are mad for you," the voices cry.

5.   "*Sic euntem per virecta pulchra odora et musica / Ales amnis
aura lucus flos et umbra iuverat.*" "Oh, mother," she wrote,
"it's too lovely here. You can't imagine. There's so much yet
to…gutters…preserves…." Their bellies some salvation in
turquoise. "What do you hear from Reverend Soames, the
Whit Sunday picnic?" Oriental nights steeped in impressions of
les arbres exotiques. "It was perfectly radiant," she wrote, "we
were as gods adrift in the lodges of our own sensations."

6.   Thicket. Hatchet. Bundle of stakes. The so-called mind's
capacity for florid self-representation. The idea of thought, for
instance. Snowberries. The holes you plug. Amnesia as
birthright. "The lemon trees," he inscribed, "of Malaga," inviting
random projection. Roof moss. Post rot. Wild rose. Salvia. "It
is a sort of contest to see who can massacre more…." Catalan
our syllables flirted with. Someone knew Lenin's name; we sliced
up the testicles on the news.

7.   The hole his love bores. The song she fell through. Worn limbs.
        A hedge-row, a spinney's green light bulbs. Its gap. Tunnel. Its
        glistening rails. Honey sweetness. "We walked down to the point," she
        wrote, "…watched tiny waves lassoing the moon. Oh mother, it's so…."
        He tore out what was weak and replaced it.

8.   The failing husband regularly drove his wife to the verdant
        previous location. In the bombed out market town the Caudillo's
        boys laboured through the night to fill in craters for the
        international press.

"News on the March!"

ATLANTIC CITY. — FASHION'S IN THE SWIM AS THESE
TWO-YEAR-OLD TWIN TOTS TAKE TO THE BEACH FOR A
WELL-SUPERVISED DAY IN THE SUN!

THEY'RE QUITE LITERALLY...HAVING A BALL!

IT SEEMS THERE'S NOTHING THESE FASHION-CONSCIOUS
YOUNGSTERS WON'T TRY WHEN IT COMES TO PLEASING
THE BOYS!

OOPS, WAKE UP, UNCLE HARRY. SAY CHEESE! OR SHOULD
THAT BE...UNCLE?

LOOKS LIKE MUM'S THE ONE WHO NEEDS A VACATION.
WELL, MUM, BETTER LUCK NEXT YEAR!

*

SPAIN. — WEEKS OF BLOODY FIGHTING COME TO AN END
AS LOYALISTS LAY SIEGE TO THE CAPITAL!

THE SKY IS BLACK WITH SOPHISTICATED NAZI BOMBERS
AS THOUSANDS OF TONS OF AERIAL EXPLOSIVES POUR
DOWN ON THE UNDISCIPLINED RED ARMIES AND THEIR
LAST-DITCH SUPPORTERS.

THOUSANDS FLEE THE LETHAL ONSLAUGHT OF THE
GENERALISSIMO'S CRACK LEGIONNAIRES! THIS LITTLE
FELLOW DIDN'T MAKE IT.

AFTER ALMOST THREE YEARS OF STUBBORN RESISTANCE,
THE COMMUNISTS ARE ON THE RUN!

CANADA. — SAY, TALK ABOUT FAR FROM THE MADDENING
CROWD, IF THIS ISN'T PARADISE WE DON'T KNOW WHAT
IS.

THE FELLOW WHO BUILT THIS PLACE LIVED LIKE A KING.
GET A WHEELBARROW LOAD OF THAT FIREPLACE!

THIS APPLE IS BIG ENOUGH TO NEED GRAVY, AND
THERE'S PLENTY MORE WHERE THAT CAME FROM!

A SPORTING GAME OF CROQUET IS JUST THE THING FOR A
LAZY SUMMER AFTERNOON. TEA FOR TWO? MAKE THAT
THREE, AND ONE FOR FIDO!

SOME LOCAL BRAVES DROP BY FOR A POW-WOW. WATCH
IT, SHORTY, THAT STOGIE WILL STUNT YOUR GROWTH!

YES, THERE'S NO DOUBT ABOUT IT, THIS VANCOUVER
ISLAND SANCTUARY DEMONSTRATES THE UNREMITTING
POPULARITY OF "NEGATIVE CAPABILITY" WITH THE YOUTH
OF TODAY!!!

30

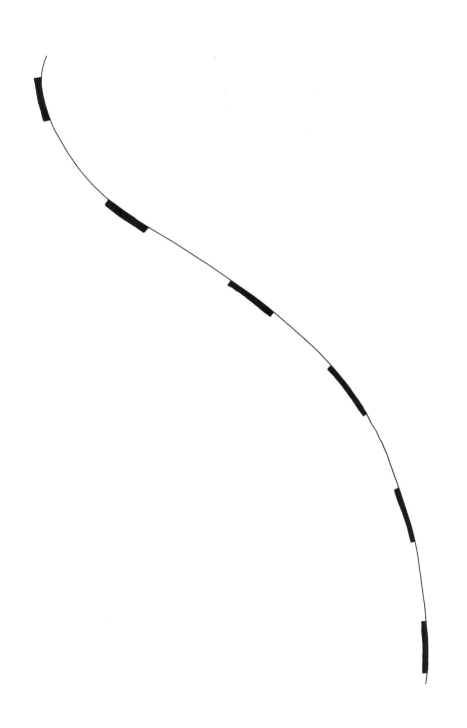

V (Blue Plate)

1. Than figs. Than sky. Than eyes. Than those. Chipped. An
    ankle. Hired as a local moron. Learning to be grateful animals.

2. There was the usual botched surfeit. Decamping to the
    basement as a wafer of inebriated fury. Than hi. Than ho.
    Than buckos for the Empire. Than his boyhood Jesus. His
    unused fragmentation bomb.

3. A boot. A basin. A vanishing subject rolling on that green.
    Tiles. Trays. Beams. Sparks. It was meant to be "home."
    Mother was savage in this way.

4. The picturesque as deflection. Light, the green hemlock
    fowling tools. Scrubbed puttees. A Camperdown Elm for
    loveliness and pretension, a little blue river rubbing by it
    through spirea. Grapes. Yellow plums. Quince. As the sky. As
    that river.

5. As he'd have it. As you were. Stand easy. As you were. Stand
    easy. Than sand. Than water. Than flight. The Major's
    regimental trousers, for instance. His mufti. A weakness for
    turbaned men. The crypt. The Scotties.

6. Leon. Zamora. Salamanca. Valladolid. Valencia. Brunete.
    Belchite. Barcelona. The smoke. The sexual quick. Names,
    more names. Prayers. A surplus of tin-pot convictions.

7. Than Teruel. Than Effie's Point. Than funnels. Than tunics.
    Than her mail home. Than her leave-taking. Than they are in
    memory, which is to say—swallowed in the current—his body,
    which is to say, this garden, this garden's suffocating walls.
    Than Figueras. Than Boadilla. Than Arganda. Than Badajoz.
    Than his

8.   Another stove-in Jerusalem. Eluding him and it. Pound—then and then. Over the mountain passes in the grassy hair of spectral children. Men in half-light. Eden. A fantasy garden, or late-blooming Falangist hybrid. In the end, what concedes to authority. Touch me as I disarm.

9.   As each day. As hatches shrank. Amnesia. On the floor lay a mysterious grey dirt which neither saw light nor considered itself an anthropomorph. Men in half-light. Tomb. Tunnel. Her wings. When she left.

10. Everything. A blur. A clot. A tunnel of twigs, hedges, holes. Thick lapels. Immaculate dogma. Petal weapons abandoned. He ruled in splendour, a Ton Ton Macoute of the heart.

11. Jew-free commerce lured him. The restoration of class-determined distribution. A wilderness with regulations; obedient fruit; pusser manhood; purity; perfectibility. Heartland. He ruled in splendour, a Ton Ton Macoute of the heart.

12. The Caudillo looked good to oak and olive. Its orange dust cover paled to apricot in the afternoon. We'd say yes too. One broke and ran. "It was hot and smelled lovely, the roses, the wild roses burst open all one afternoon like a swarm of eels." For a while it had been not wisteria, not clematis but home. So much home to haul about.

13. Someone remembered her. Heads rained down. "She was very nice, she'd always say hello." Nature, or fiction. That's it. A spoon of stars at Effie's Point. Swollen berry tips. He ruled in splendour. Heads rained down. She'd always say hello. So much hello to haul about. When she went she went for keeps.

VI (Cedar File)

1.   The song she fell through. The hole her head sang. The hole his song held. The field she fell through. The head her hole held. The head he fell through. The fall his song sang. The song her hole held. The hole he fell through. The field his head held. The hole his song sang. The head she fell through.

2.   This is how the narrative begins: "We swam stripped at Effie's Point. There was no house there then. Swimmer's hearts took heart in the narrow trail, the surge of gumflower and honeysuckle and arbutus bells…." This is how it begins. It concludes, "In war one becomes a jackal." Well, not exactly. It concludes, "It was lovely; it was neither paradise nor memory nor any mystic lexicon we adore." Wrong again. It concludes with a double space above the footnote rule.

3.   Before us it was so lovely, and there was nothing before us. *"Vedi lo sol che 'n fronte ti riluce; / vedi l'erbette, i fiori e li arbuscelli / che qui la terra sol da sé produce."* On wings, a mote, the sexual thickness. She must have been encouraged by the potential for gooseberries. Jelly. Cards. Thorn. Runnels in the dark.

4.   The single path. The single hole. The single wood she fell through. *"…la divina foresta spessa e viva…."*

5.   Fraught husk. Her *Lifes* stacked in trunks. The regimental photographs coming alive each night and parading through her china. Everyone then was someone else, without a body. In his elegant, vindictive house-to-house, hand-to-hand reverie he mopped up the boulevards of Madrid. He tossed moss off. He burned tents down. He stuffed envelopes. Once no one came and was someone. She noticed the sky take light. Then she walked down to the sea.

6.   Forged ardour. Forest harder. For his daughter. For her stutter. For Erse udder. For a shudder. For a shed her father urged her. Forearms, head a farther merger. Forearmed, hedged a far merganser. "Marry me," she said. He ground her under.

7.   *"Intrate; ma facciovi accorti*
che di fuor torna chi 'n dietro si guata."

[The music of the firestorm begins.]

VII (The Sea)

[The Firestorm ceases it roaring and turns to embers. Over the embers we hear the SW radio, followed by fragments of the distorted Orphée melody with the river's current running through it. The river is the Hebrus, into which Orphée's head was tossed; it's also the Ebro in Spain and, of course, one of the four rivers of Paradise which flood the sea and girdle the world as Okeanos.]

1. Smoke, then; a flare. Sheds. Beams. Slat light. Ripples. Hard tunic. Fingers. A reservoir. Out there Okeanos, a hole in you. Head of a man thrown to pigs. The river at his temples.

2. Yes, you—hole in the river, hole in the thicket, hole in the telling you're told through. Head of you afloat in the gash your tongue tore. "*...hermosura viril / que en montes de carbón, anuncios y ferrocarriles, / soñabas ser un río y dormir como un río....*" Rubber of your own unrolling....

3. *"Vengo a buscar lo que busco,*
    mi alegría y mi persona."

    "I come in search of what I am seeking,
    my joy and my own self."

4. Father, is that you? Is that your cold head twisting in the river? And have we gathered here before? And the great steel bridge at Mora? Is that us—there, together?

5.   "*...eese de meen krupsasa loho...*

"...his mother sent him
into a hidden place of
ambush...

                                         "*...enethake de herseen arpan
karharodonta,*

"...placed into his hands
a jagged-toothed sickle,

                                         "*...dolon d'upethakato panta.*"

"...and instructed him fully
in the whole deceit."

                                         "...in his hands the jagged-
toothed sickle...."

6.   "*...hombre solo en el mar,*" dismembered man. Father, I
swallowed that part of you to make this river to bring you here.
Now will you forgive me?

+ + +

7.   All is lovely movement on the water, squall and cross-squall—a
slick—then lift and fall. A shiver. It makes you weep, "*Agonía,
agonía, sueño, fermento y sueño. Este es el mundo, amigo,
agonía, agonía.*" Paradise is built on agonía. From its garden
we're strewn, its gates restrain and quicken us; its melodious
tongues deliver us—all, all, in sweet, sweet *agonía.* Hand-
shaped, heart-shaped, haven-shaped....

8. Thicket. Hatchet. Bundle of twigs. The little head gleams. The
    hole its singing pierces, the hole it sings itself through….
    Passwords, tesserae, incantations…. A flush. *HOMETEGIMA
    UMUD IO OC TECROG NO LAMBEC ACICLUEG FOMMELAMMUDOG
    GECABAG GOM IC MUE NEMTUM LETE IC MUE LEC AIOD
    LATAMANA. ICA NACA NO TIMEG AGURA DAG MANOMAG. OCSE
    A BIGLAM DE BIGLE TU ADOMUA TU OMGECA…. ASECUA,
    ASECUA…. OGRO OG OD TICNE, ATUSE, ASECUA, ASECUA….*
    Thicket. Tunnel. Hatchet of twigs. Breach. Hand-shaped,
    heart-shaped, haven-shaped….

9. *"…te, dulcis coniunx, te solo in litore,*
    te veniente die, te decedente…."

           "…you, sweet wife, you alone on the desolate shore,
           you at the coming of day, you at its passing…."

10. What ground endures. What hunger perishes. What perishes.
    What hungers. What consumes. What swills. What shits. What
    beguiles. What denies. What clings. What corrupts. What
    ennobles. What enslaves. What rewards. What impoverishes.
    What enriches. What rots. What nourishes. What penetrates.
    What fetters. What forsakes. What resists. What preserves.
    What forgives. What chips, hacks stone, roots honeysuckle in
    its cracks. Nectar of paradise: how it grips us—its articulate
    fragrance, its seductive palisades, its wistful economy of
    agonía. Enough! I spit on your paradise. Father, I call you
    sickle and hurl myself upon you.

                                              8 July 1989
                                              Vancouver, B.C.

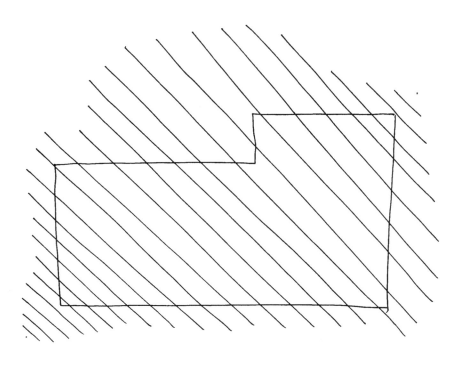

Arguably Vaccine

Drive on recent tools
fester's bite drills dear
hornswoggling's custom rule
rubs rocks warm.

Arguably vaccine
these finer hairs
scoundrels part in tune.
A file of lads I stood in stood.

The lump heaves pores
up. In toxic soap
a Mickey waves. Pa
you can't just go like this.

+

Weep on select infants
heads, bullets, your beck
the rot from what I've not
got runs my heart.

Drill clean, viral
staircase. The Tommy's
the measure of the Angel. Quick,
sing radiator, recall some

thing to thing
deepest feeling felt right
now a little chickadee's
or

+

waiting. And she
when
    to
                  for

       by
          in
at
                         with

      from
           wi

                             January 1991

Blondin!

Look up.
That is no petal.

i

Blondin! The café's curated macaroni's rue distracts. No one mentions smallpox. A post-adolescent sweeper fears *"character reference."* Blondin, your long wand trembles over the whirlpool. You complete the sky!
The lovers are not frisky tonight
(affectionate designates the bulk of most filters). Ambulance's telephoto creep on that grainy curve along Dog Lake seems
a mirage, or is that a decoy?
We stood on our anymore. Toes for that plum and they were.

ii

His dream: "I stood by the great Falls, overpowered by its terrible sublimity.
    Suddenly my clothing dropped from my form as if by magic and
    before me, across the boiling flood, was stretched a silken cord
    as delicate as a thread of gossamer."

iii

— "Papa, why are the angels so miserable?"

iv

It's with Foreman and Longman on the brow (Tommy Tinker).
— "What's your name?"
— "What's yours?"
— "Blondin! I complete the sky!"

v

The compelling threat of devotion.

vi

I've got the kid dick-deep in a canal hidden by a hippo-sized rock. That one
the ring road rings. I've got George & Vic funambulizing on a bridge and
a jeer slicing them. Remember? "Quick, quick, see if you can!"
Bridge, book, sinking *'of'*. That was thirty years ago. How many
dinners can you reconstruct? Boltanski's clay cod.
Twigs for carrots. Teeming brain.
Homage to sage.

vii

Suckers for duopanauroflorageoacoustikalmicroobservationism we note
each stone and stamen.
— "Talk him, talk him."
— "Look. The sun's out."
I re
— "Look, there's Tink!" I turn my wrist.

A disk of light zips out the door.

viii

Tearing off the ivory Turkish pantaloons, the plum vest, the wig, the skull cap, he stepped off the platform at White's Pleasure Grounds and within moments, attired in flesh-coloured tights and shirt, he was standing out over the Falls.

"Lord of the Hempen Realm!"

ix

The professor is designating a line to punch *punctum* in even as this morning morning's market maintains its "flight to quality."

Soon it was with stilts, with peach baskets lashed to his feet, with headstands and one hand and by his knees, with a stove to fry an omelette on, a plate and cutlery to eat it with, and, on a dark summer night, with fizgigs and whirligigs and Roman candles,
he harrowed the hell-pit of Niagara.

x

Don't ever give in.

xi

Look way up.
Susanna. I hold you in one hand high above my head and you're so pleased, so standing there—my fingers cupped, gripping your toes—proud. Blondin! Always be that.

xii

— "*Invisible?* Oh, you mean invisible?"

Tipping Over

Situation demands an organ wheezes to a stop and clapped hands
rise, wither; night's joint flaps. The sweet hill's

called upon to make herself presentable to commerce. Gouges and
flames of sage ignite old glands. Blind draws. Mind

thorned with hedges. So pill-box-hatted jaunties recline aussi in Degas,
serviced with fluid s landscape, chained one to each and, predictably,

their women or tailors. We flex dread in disturbing
and attractive ways, doubtless in preamble or, per Lebowitz, "blowing

smoke," as the swollen orifice is for mendacity fêted and importuned
to boost festival attendance. Interior awnings recommend

demobilization. Furious with shade, hedge-dweller bends, hips,
bellows.

Boys, let your anima pull you off! ...a burst of Harriet-fury! Wind!
It's New Year's, my sole disclosure.

January 1988

Little Pinkie

The long knotted cord of what we remember—calling (ineptly)
memory—blunts desire, or smells so. Why depend on it?

Chuck it.
What's its forsaking moraine? Neutrinos, Tang-coloured

on an eyelid's band shell? Buggy herms? Air, or what
passes for it? Are these not heritaginous? As your cracked hands?

The starlings in the eaves she turns her head to, sucking in her air,
is that not animal joy? People are bored; yes, that's why

they turn to real estate. Their memories fail them, they say (foreclosure).
So much remains to be simulated. Some await the perfect quarto, jupe

or teeth. I've supposedly woken to imagine my tiny restless daughter in a
teenage pink ski jacket with hair like Farah Fawcett. It could be otherwise;

it could be Brian Fawcett. But, seriously folks, you stride into the tawny
parlour, draw down that aluminum sleeve, those three shiny flat legs, hinge

the screen as if it were a Viking sail, empower the humming utility, and
there you are—large as life—drowned in class struggle. Note the grimace,

the selfless compromise, the gesture of goodwill which proved you a fool.
Betray your origins and they'll betray you. Little Pinkie, I love you willfully

and without circumference, whoever we are. No questions asked. You teach
the light to dance: "...*e fuor di quella / è defettivo ciò ch'è lì perfetto.*"

I salute your Romanian undershirts.

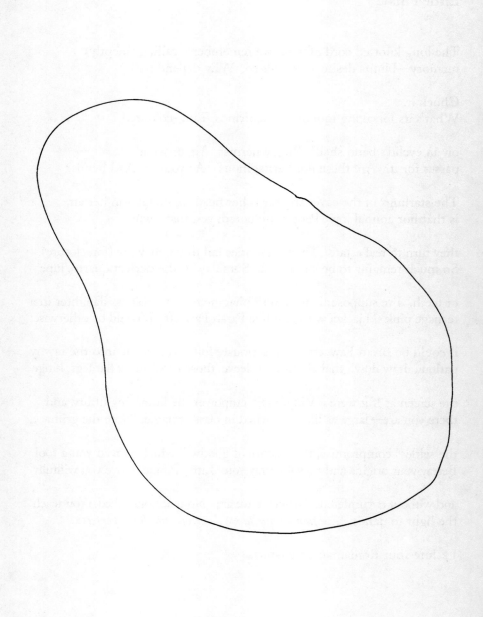

The Dam

For my sister on her 30th birthday

August 18, 1979

algae sing
in ponds
ur–dragonflies
climb fronds…

we swam
all ears
in Marge's
dam deep

black water
filled from
punctured springs
cold toes

told rufus
hummingbirds sipped
at lichen
clarinets alders

their leaning
admired
bass between
them stitching

silver bubble
trails dragonflies
buzz sawyered
over heads

white legs
dangled amber
laugh you
choked and

sank into
the loamy
bag of
memory water

how sensational
to drift
all ivory
through flakes

of golden
bark and
feathered algae
how pleasing

the plonk
of bullfrogs
breaststroking by
a tumbled

log they
sun on
how intoxicating
oneself to

sun in
buttercups and
hot grass
flicking tadpoles

with idle
fingers of
gold watching
waterbeetles dart

where? who
knows I
never found
out though

I built
the wharf
one summer
morning pounding

four by
fours into
the ligneous
forest floor

up to
my amber
waist in
water nailing

planks from
bank to
piling tops
trying it

out diving
into the
cold part
the shore

unable to
hold me
longer now
Marge how

do you
like it?
Two things
I'd made

with my
hands both
failures both
novelties but

this this
wharf the
summer the
swimmers everyone

was counting
on a
wharf it
was absolutely

vital Marjorie
would have
to give
up swimming

without it
Well Marge
what do
you think?

It's good
it's very
good it's
just what

we need
her knees
wobbling on
jagged stones

her life
depending on
the wharf
sliding shoulder

high she
pushed away
gliding out
across the

dam with
reflections playing
in her
white hair

gliding in
a water
beetle's V
and reversing

noiselessly across
the memory
bag ivory
skinned with

gold rippling
on her
fingers not
a sound

but frogs
plonking and
Taffy snuffling
in a

weasel hole
snapping willow
twigs startling
mallards into

a flap
the mysterious
splash of
your own

lurch forward
Seems strong
enough eh?
Yes it

will last
as long
as I
need it

swimming ashore
to dry
herself in
the sun

smoke a
cigarette before
another supper
and later

when sun
was lost
to the
other side

and the
drake swam
emboldened by
silence I

ran back
jingling with
spikes from
Bevil's' tins

shiplap and
a saw
to labour
among dragonflies

in last
light fastening
my wharf
to forever.

Trio

I Masquerade, Then

It is never never reducible. Oleander is only one
of them and faded or was said to as they all do
fade as glads as glads do too glads because she on
the phone at dawn thought glads hand him me me too
a glad too a second blooming

II Instinctual

Inveterate card she card she hooded
hooded she handed she intemperate
hand she her way she handed hooded
hood she she handed she winked she
from to to bedded winked here she she woe
invertebrate

III Decked

Cargo I know I can see (it) I says
I can I know I I I I do I we
woe me deck we cargo on on

September 1989

Lunatick Bawling

"They mayntayne theire lyfe by sekinge theire deathe."

Sir Thomas More, "on Warfare",
Utopia, the Second Book.
Trans. Raph Robynson (1556)

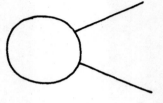

"To make of a long siege a short narration..."
Richard Hakluyt

1

The wild potato boasts twelve gates too. A hedge-fetish—the *"dear old flag"*—
endures. A coarse screen from a purportedly prize-winning photo-essay has
"artist" incarcerated in Tyrolean psychiatric institution. Yes. His wraiths, their
limbs and trunks stylized, overlap. He is wondering, is he a mine-layer or a
mine-sweeper? Tolerable attenuation. Old Testament his hunch hinges to.
He grows younger there as you decay, his desiccation stymied (his enviable
visage). Some host, your savage organ. And on a night like this.

2

Empire's absent until page 60, long past *cock-a-doodle-do*, *oo-oo* and *tumpa-
tum-too*. Here, on 135, *queer*. *Queer/pot*. Broadacre City, predicted Wright,
would "revive emasculated manhood." Marvell's *Cramp of Hope*. Is it
peristaltic then?

3

We've our blocks unboxed; we're building the City again, its temple rising above
the river banks in Gothic caps. We're at it every day now its lilac hedge,
anemones, the barracks, its sticky gates, πυλῶν—ah, like a bride then?
He (heeling to custom) counsels, "An angel finds a man." We are always doing
this, hefting shaft and beam, bottle and quoin, this x that, that x that, our
lonesome Nauvoos scented with brain hyssop and mulberry. Imperium. I am
ravished in thee potential new bushes.

4

There is a flesh-coloured succulent that springs from the fossils fully formed, we're told, outside the walls. Raw, moist, smudged fuschia for a throat, it withers by nine. Perhaps I have never been able to rise early enough to watch it burst through the shale.

5

    "One evening Patty said, 'Tomorrow will be Empire Day. Will there be a parade?'
    'Yes,' said Father, 'there will be a big parade tomorrow.'
    'We shall all go in our car and carry the beautiful old flag that Grandfather gave me.'"

6

What for febrifuge? For gargling? For cancers? For warts? Variola? What Extractum Humorale, Arum Potabile, Panchimagogum, St. Hugh's bones in store? What minarets? What currents in cotoneaster? And who, pray, for Zapoletes? And to the Virgin? The chief is asking for consolation.

7

In the square twelve pearls: Fang Lizhi, Li Shuxian, Ran Wanding, Weng Zhengming, Yao Yongzhan and more. You know their names. We are building the temple arm in arm again. Banners fly and I shall hear you singing my beloved, your song reeling in memories, μετανοει, *we are bearing witness.* "An angel finds a man." We would not choose the scented wilderness unless we wanted to sleep beneath trees, to be woken by swallows. I am game. Father will you hunt me?

8

That is one explanation. "Look," said the young guy at the municipal zoo, "women are flying!"

And the Tyrolean spa? The jade altars? The wild geranium at the gate? The corn-leaf dolly?

9

Day and night they gather, these pilgrims set sail from Spurn Point, Van Dieman's Land and others. It's uncomplicated. Their campfires have stolen the stars. A toot or is it an *oo-oo* suffices to say you can leave your worries here on this doorstep, one of twelve, say. What were you reading back in '46, papa? *Tumpa-tumpa-too.* Such talk about the water, its loveliness, always its loveliness, what can it mean to us again, huddled as we are against it? Numen. You're looking into the sky too as if it could ever be your placenta.

10

"An angel finds a man."

We are stupid with hope. Could it be our diet?

11

"Empire Day came, but Father could not be in the parade. He had to go to another town.
He said, 'I am sorry that I must go today.' Then he said good-bye and went away in the car."
O.H.M.S.

12

So your kings sallied forth, by the Grace of God our only God, Maker and Preserver of all Things and Replenisher of All Things, Richard, John, Henry, their lords and dukes and all, your monks and charlatans, soldiers, strumpets and hymn-humming tar-and-featherers, your gartered Earls, C.S.M.'s, R.S.M.'s, profiters from misery, thugs and tire-slashers, child despoilers, clowns, gang-heroes, village bullies, cheek-lickers, welt-suckers, toadies of all stripes, eel-swallowers, boil gourmets, face-lifters, pimps, parade-prancers, politicians, priests, pontiffs and their seed-miserly tribe, those unsavoury of breath, the cowards, the craven, the frigid, the vain, the pompous, the virtuous, the self-absorbed, the navigators, the liars, the prigs of righteousness, grave-pickers, nose-pickers, nit-pickers, all manner of snickerers and swine, civil and uncivil servants, housewives, midwives, husbands, daughters, dog-beaters, sorcerers, anthem-howlers, vicious swabs, flag-wavers, traitors, precious beauties, scum and honest toilers; all on, on with henna and cymbals to the Holy City—lunaticks all!

13

And is it built with sticks? The angels' ribs, are they sticks? Do we place the yew, the rowan trees so, to make it like home? And is the first gate gallows too?

December 1989

Five Translations

In collaboration with Qiu Xia He

Performed at the Hornby Festival, August 3 & 4, 1991

Many thanks to Tom Durrie

Li Po, "Saying Goodbye, On the Road to Shu"

The road goes straight up.
Hold tight.
Keep your cheek to the inside wall.
Climb, climb until your horse's ears burst
through the clouds. Far below the plank roads
snake between the trees.
Rivers shimmer on the dark plain of Shu.
Old friend, what more is there to know?
What use would a fortune-teller be?

Li Po, "Lady Wang Chao-Jun - I"

Chao-Jun is taking the pearl saddle!
See how she touches them.
Her cheeks are little too red.
Tonight she is one of us; tomorrow, his.

Li Po, "Lady Wang Chao-Jun - II"

In Han the Han moon was her companion.
One night it clung to her, its shadow grew long and thin;
the next morning she was gone.

That night the Han moon pierced the sky.
In a strange, far-off city, a western moon rises on a bride's bolted shutters.
In that place, they say, the flowers are made of snow.

They buried her in the sand.
I remember her eyebrows. Who does not?
As for our lives? We've no portrait painter to blame.
Her tomb is a green blip in the western desert. The wind howls.
You would too if you were there.

Tu Fu, "Visiting an Ancient Site"

Mountains, valleys, mountains, valleys, on it goes until you reach the village
        where Ming-fei was born.
She once climbed the great staircase in the crimson evening air;
now she pushes up weeds in the stupid northern desert.
Bells chime, the gingko flutters.
It almost seems she's among us still.
Perhaps it's only the wind.
But year after year her song is sung. When you hear the pi-pa play
you can't help but get the blues.

Tu Fu, "Jia-Ren"

Something about her.
Something about the poky little river town I found her in.
She eats what she scrounges in her garden and sells the rest each fall when
      she pulls in her skirts for winter.
Do you remember the rebels in Chang'an, up in the high passes?
Two of them were her brothers and they got caught.
She did everything she could. The buggers stalled until the bodies
of those two boys had to be peeled off their stakes and pitched into the river.
No burial, no funeral.
Some new order!
They wait till you're down.
Don't think you'd be any different.
Her old man, a regular windsock, took off with another woman.
I don't know, trees seem to behave themselves,
ducks have no trouble being faithful,
but this guy went nuts over his new squeeze;
he was blind to anything else.
You know how it is. In the mountains the water's crystal clear;
in the valley all turns conveniently muddy…
Now her servant carries her pearls to the market, one by one.
Jia-Ren spends hours stuffing twigs into holes in the roof.
Why, she asked me, should she seek out flowers for her hair?
These days, she says, she's as likely to wear a handful of bullrushes.
Then she trembles in her thin blue shirt
in the stunted bamboo grove.

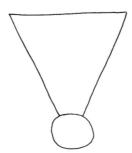

Salt? Scrape.

Listen to your wild fascination with yourself.
I laud your repugnant efforts and watch
the long shadow under your leg. Would you kneel with me?
The child I do in.
I trust these are not boredom lesions *à la* the winery hound?
So that now what you loved too well is commercially attainable you can have it.

Harshest reserve for a comma; veneer sparkles in comparison. That coarsely-screened photogenic boreal appliqué she took my hand in her tiny fingers under and in her simultaneously Heidi/Gepetto vocalization chirping, "Papa, a reconnaissance satellite!"

You may think of it as a small furry animal skidding in and out of a horizontal burrow. Along the upper left hand side a coherent slick of ferric oxide crystals in a binding medium registers the creature's vital signs pendant ingress/egress.

Call it Paradiso. Heart's own tourist bureau.

Hear the complicated military gestures of your beloved. What upstairs?

And that sweet infant sleeping out there in Vancouver. Always pressing, here.

Arresting program, this. Sensitive prerequisite, augmenting corpse with pupae. And the scenery!

One wanted to be a Holy Fool and most would say he made it.
To slip through being, hiss between what could be and could be.

Blondin = Eros!
Pindar = The dream of a sh(ad)ow.
Medium = grove.
Text = trench.
Eye = hedge
Ram = time.
Ewe = I.

Bark, ore, ash, soil. Slops.
Bundles of twigs, the river's reeds, its song his shape they carve in clay.
You begin at the throat.
Listen for his rattle.

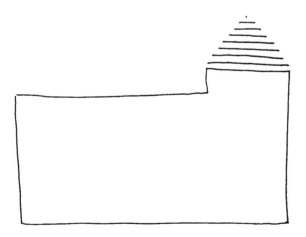

Father

A He I've The and

year has his the

later not glasses I hair

and been slid cuttings

a here his from in

day or sword his

He here nose

flap was or of

here here white

and paper

here

14 September 1996

Altar

A Working Narration for a Film

(1999)

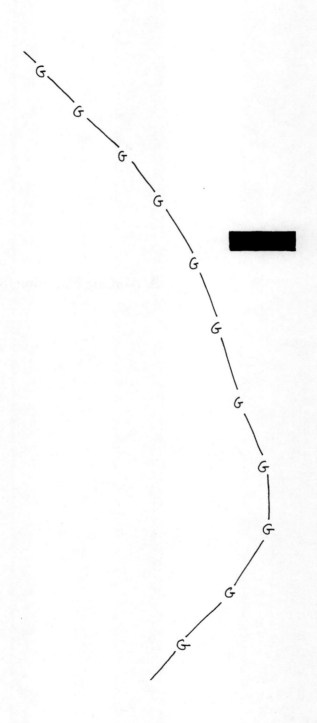

Introductory song: Richard Strauss, op. 27, No. 4

*M*_{orgen!}

And tomorrow the sun will shine again
and on the path I shall follow
it will again unite us, joyfully,
on this sun-breathing earth...

And we shall go down quietly and slowly
to the wide shore, with its blue waves;
speechless, we shall gaze into each other's eyes
and on us will fall the mute silence of bliss...

John Henry Mackay (1894)

What is left to forget?
Language has swept us all away.

Did we not want freedom?
Did we not want to unload ourselves of ourselves forever?

On our way down Skull Rock, latitude 49° 30', longitude 123° 20'. September. My daughter Susanna is five. There is no hand-holding.

Dry moss and yellow grass grow from the cracks and ledges that plunge to the sea. The causeway, a jawbone of boulders far below us, is dark with foam.

But it is sunny and windy halfway down the face of Skull Rock and I try to revive our pirate game. Her friend is laughing; I reach for her hand. Susanna slithers by us to a clump of snowberry. She hits a patch of shiny grass and slips from view.

I lurch forward. A scrawny little juniper has broken her fall. She has seized the trunk with her fingers and hangs there as if she'd planned it all along.

She looks up at me.

"Dad," she says, giving me a chance to catch my breath, "Dad, if I *fell* you'd go ahead of me and be there so I could fall on you; you'd catch me, wouldn't you, so I wouldn't hurt myself?"

This with an eye on her friend.

An editorial from the *Times* of London, March 8th, 1919, not quite a year after my father was born: "*…discipline to an army is what honour is to a woman. Once lost it can never be restored.*"

Across the hall a woman is shouting. "They should have told me! Please don't save me!"

On the river, round pebbles in the yellow cut-banks.

Do you know the story of Sedna? Every man for miles around wanted to marry her, but she turned them down, one by one. Her father was furious. He instructed her to marry the next man who came to the door.

Before too long a handsome stranger knocked on the heavy door. Sedna obeyed her father. She married the young man and consoled herself with the thought that he was not as ugly or ill-suited as some. After a terrifying journey on the icy sea she arrived at the barren rock where the young man lived. As he stepped ashore he changed his shape. It was Storm Petrel.

He led Sedna to their new home, a nest of sticks strewn with fish skins, bones and soiled feathers. The wind howled. Sedna remained loyal to her father, and did her best to make a new life as Storm Petrel's mate. More than once she regretted her stubbornness.

After a year her father realized his mistake and set out to rescue his daughter, searching all the islands in the ocean. He found her at last, squatting in the evil-smelling nest on the barren rock, and they set off together for home.

Returning at sunset, Storm Petrel discovered that Sedna had betrayed him. He flew out to sea where he found and attacked their kayak. The father paddled backward and forward, trying to outrun the shrieking bird. A storm blew up. The boat was taking on water.

With his life in peril, the father grabbed Sedna and flung her into the sea, crying, "She's your wife, take her!"

Sedna tried to climb back in beside him, but he brought his paddle down on her fingers—Wham! He shattered off the first joints. These fell into the ocean and became seals. Sedna tried once more to climb in and he slashed at her fingers again, this time severing them at the second joint. These dropped into the ocean to become walruses. Once again she pleaded for her father's mercy, but he continued to smash and smash at her fingers, this time slicing off the third joints, which dove to the bottom of the sea to become whales.

Sedna followed, corkscrewing through the living darkness.

In the yellow sand-banks, pale blue stones.

"The Soldier's Dilemma"

"*It is sometimes alleged that obedience to Military Law may be in conflict with a soldier's duty as an ordinary citizen...a soldier is required by Military Law to obey the commands of his superior officer. This obligation extends only to lawful commands; and a soldier is not liable in military law for disobeying an unlawful order. But how is the soldier to judge the lawful character of the order? He has not the time to weigh up its merits, even if he has the inclination and the ability to do so. His training makes compliance instinctive. Unlawful injury, inflicted as the result of such compliance, renders him liable to criminal and civil proceedings. He cannot plead obedience to the order of his military superior, because no such defence is accepted by a civil court. If the order of the superior is, in the soldier's opinion, unlawful, he disobeys it at the peril of being court-martialled for a serious military offence, and runs the risk of the court-martial not accepting his view of the order's unlawful character. Moreover, unless the order is wholly unreasonable, it would prejudice military discipline, if strict compliance were not enforced by military law. A soldier, therefore, ought to obey orders, at the peril of civil proceedings being instituted against him for the resulting act. If such proceedings result from obedience to the order there is some authority for saying that, if the order is not manifestly unlawful, he cannot be made liable.*"

What is left to forget? Hazel-grove, anemone?

The air pushed forward by your shuffling in the halls. Your hair, thin and yellow, your sweet smile, your lips in need of Vaseline, your stoop. Your curiosity—deferential—preoccupied with something beyond us: the voice between two clouds, a keyhole in Barbara Stanwyck's hair, acrobats, running lights, continents of trembling and glory, the bright shaking of poplars.

I carry the hair I clipped from your scalp that starry night in March when you slipped away between the trees. I used the pair of Chinese gun-metal scissors attached to the key chain. I want to say *flew away* between the trees.

Bright shaking of poplars...

Bezalel, son of Uri, hammered the vessels from new bronze: the pots, the shovels, the tossing-bowls, the forks, the fire pans.

"*The basin and its stand of bronze he made out of the bronze mirrors of the women waiting at the entrance to the Tent....*"

In this basin Aaron's sons were washed. In their "*turban(s) of fine linen, the tall headdresses and their bands all of fine linen, the shorts of finely woven linen, and the sashes of finely woven linen, embroidered in violet, purple, and scarlet,*" they established the hereditary priesthood, standing erect before the basin of plundered mirrors.

The pasture rises over the creek behind the I.C. Unit. Jump across in the sun, in the cold air: swollen canes, yellow bark, your disappearing footprint in the gravel and up the far bank onto the high field beyond where the wind rattles the wires. Four firs ascend out of the thicket, two on either side, the pillars of a gate.

Cross here; cross through; spring over gurgle and gleam, up onto the high field, Dad. Wave-light in hay, wind-hammered gold, this scuttle no metaphor but a true thing.

Juniper, crocus, ocean spray.

"*Every person subject to military law who commits any of the following offences; that is to say,*

(1) Shamefully abandons or delivers up any garrison, place, post, or guard, or uses any means to compel or induce any governor, commanding officer, or other person shamefully to abandon or deliver up any garrison, place, post, or guard, which it was the duty of such governor, officer, or person to defend; or

(2) Shamefully casts away his arms, ammunition, or tools in the presence of the enemy; or

(3) Treacherously holds correspondence with or gives intelligence to the enemy, or treacherously or through cowardice sends a flag of truce to the enemy; or...."

"*The world is a corpse-eater. All the things eaten in it themselves die also.*

Truth is a life-eater."

I asked the learned professor to tell me what he knew about recent events in the mountains. It was a delicate subject; could he speak freely?

I recalled to him the volcano's green flank as the sun fell away, its analytical shadows.

In the dour city (latitude 1° 20', longitude 77° 15'), life had returned to normal, but I'd had the distinct impression from the moment of my arrival that I was witnessing an impressive dumb show, that each man, woman and child, bound by duty, was acting out a vital role in an austere, joyless pantomime. Not one foot was out of place; not one stitch was dropped.

At first I thought my imagination must be enflamed by the fever and amoebic bleeding.

A boast in a café, for instance, proferred by a new acquaintance, would without warning fold itself inside out and shatter in mid-air. A fraction of a second before the shattering the entire room, that is to say all those sprawled about me in attitudes of indolence or, perhaps, in a masquerade of yearning, lifted their heads as if, somewhere in the distant future, they were listening into the terrible whistle of eternity. Then a subordinate clause would sweep the conversation up off the floor and my acquaintance would chatter on as if nothing had happened at all.

On another occasion a mirror on a public scale held my likeness in its peeling bevel for a full second after I'd dismounted.

Watching an elderly man search for his hearing-aid one afternoon in the municipal swimming pool, I could have sworn he glanced quickly to either side before pulling up a corner of the foliated scene behind him. When he perceived my stare he dropped what he'd lifted and fell to examining a pile of clothes he'd twice tipped upside-down.

This incident encouraged me to accept for once the evidence of my own eyes. These earnest, energetic citizens, it appeared, devoted every moment of their lives to the task of *concealing* a world that seemingly ran *parallel* to the world I shared with them. When a mother bent to inject herself with insulin beneath a canopy of plane trees in the central plaza, for instance, an identical mother bent to inject insulin at the same angle and with the same measured pressure on the plunger under an identical canopy in the parallel world a thin scrim's distance away.

Was this a trick of mirrors—perhaps of many mirrors—like the glittering row of reflections that runs along the sink tops in a public lavatory?

One further observation. When the old man searching for his hearing aid lifted the flap of the world behind him, I perceived an identical old man behind him, tugging at the flap of his own backdrop to reveal…but what I saw there I dare not say, except to relate that it was the subject of my question to the learned professor that leafy afternoon this past summer during a not-entirely chance encounter, to which he replied, yes, it was not impossible although he was only going by what he'd been told, of course, although he clearly chose not to speak about his own experiences except to relate an anecdote about a grisly consecration held prior to building a bridge near Urubamba which seemed like common knowledge or, at least, related to a commonly-held suspicion, but soon he was chatting to me about a particular moth in his garden which was threatening his lilacs and a recent article by a colleague in an internationally-recognized medical journal on the subject of amoebic dysentery he'd be willing to translate and send my way, for which, I replied, of course, I'd be most grateful.

In the garden of the *oubliette*
there is nothing to forget;
the hedger strives to keep intact
each sunbeam, every glowing fact.

Your beak, in bed, could you hear us? Our memoirs of
indiscretions, couplings, cocktails, predatory imperialists? How the order
of things granted a visiting British officer immunity to feel up your wife
in the kitchen while his mates guzzled your booze in the living room? A
boat: the *Sine Wave*. Losing a salmon at the edge of a squall, the wives'
revenge, pictures stitched together from rugs and uniforms and uneaten
food, hair under barbers' chairs, a spring day in Ottawa in '45, your
brother showing up out of the blue. "There's nothing to drink in this
house," he said. Later on, you two exchanging uniforms, perched in the
little hallway inside the front door on Delaware Avenue demolishing a
quart of gin. Against your mother's wishes your new western wife went
out and bought more. Last year, a neighbour told me you boys had a
reputation as kids for splitting wood in the basement with a .303.
  "Mother I see thee still."

What is left to forget?

What was it you skimmed over, in school, in your textbook, that afternoon in late June, was it, four years before all hell broke loose? May I look over your shoulder?

"When the young voyager plots his course on the adventurous sea of life, and examines his chart for the ways marked easy *and* lucrative, *and his parents look over his shoulder to point out the passages of* health, safety, advancement *and* social standing, *let the mentor of life, ripe with the experience of ages, and young with the hopes of the future, speak and advise youth to nail to the masthead the pennant of service. Whether one sweeps the streets, teaches the young, or grows bread for the hungry, his occupation is created, not that he shall live, but because his is a needful work for mankind in general. Public service is the real measure of one's vocation."*

"You are the knights errant of our tragic modern world," said the Princess to the Governor-General, *"who were ready 'to ride abroad redressing human wrongs.'"*

Atropine, every three hours. Breathing hard, breathing scared. Marian's father saying of Susanna as she learned to speak words: "She's working as hard now as she'll ever work in her life."

This gasping, Dad, its rival.

Beneath pale-blue stones, feldspar; water.

"*Every person subject to military law who on active service commits any of the following offences; that is to say,*

(1) Without orders from his superior officer leaves the ranks in order to secure prisoners or horses, or on pretence of taking wounded men to the rear; or

(3) Is taken prisoner, by want of due precaution, or through disobedience of orders, or willful neglect of duty, or having been taken prisoner fails to rejoin His Majesty's service when able to rejoin same; or

(4) Without due authority either holds correspondence with, or gives intelligence to, or sends a flag of truce to the enemy; or

(6) In action, or previously to going into action, uses words calculated to create alarm or despondency; or

(7) Misbehaves or induces others to misbehave before the enemy in such a manner as to show cowardice...."

"*An Indian pupil is hard to teach. He or she rarely answers a question, and certainly never asks one. The most amusing situations never provoke a smile. Of what is the little Indian thinking when he looks straight ahead in school? Perhaps he pictures the mossy logs and murmuring streams of the deep and solemn forest, through which he glides with bow and arrow.*"

The overhang, white roots, the noise of water!

It must not be seen to be a table, although it is four square as a table is and owes its shape to—or perhaps precedes—a table. It must be made of acacia wood. The altar will inhabit the volume of a table, if not the mass of a table, without being a table, yet it must behave as a table behaves.

What else resembles this? Anything a word stands for, to begin with. Your name, you.

In the valley of moraines, egg-shaped, speckled boulders.

"*There are three main classes of immigrant: those from the United Kingdom, whom we most prefer, but who are often poor and without experience in pioneer life; those from the United States, who have sold their farms, and have moved across the border to find cheaper land; and lastly, the Europeans and Asiatics, who are foreigners in the real sense. The peoples who have come since 1901 are largely the following:*

"*British, Americans, Japanese, Austrians, Chinese, Germans, Russians, Hindus, Jews, Italians.*

"*To induce these people to come to our country, the Government spent $18,000,000, or more than five dollars for each. Steamship companies were given $4.86 for each suitable settler they secured, and half that amount for children; advertising was carried on in the main centres of Europe, and agents in the United States received $3 per man, $2 per woman and $1 per child, on genuine settlers for Western Canada.*"

"Please father," she cries, "I didn't do anything. Help me, please, I didn't do nothing. I pray to the Lord I never did. As God is my judge I never did. Somebody please help me, I didn't do nothin'."

"...*to make the castle of Liebenstein fast and impregnable, a child was bought for hard money of its mother and walled in. It was eating a cake while the masons were at work, the story goes, and it cried out, 'Mother, I see thee still,' then later, 'Mother, I see thee a little still;' and, as they put in the last stone, 'Mother, now I see thee no more.'"*

Oh, the red-tipped grasses!

"*Every person subject to military law who commits any of the following offences; that is to say*

(1) Causes or conspires with any other persons to cause mutiny or sedition in any of His majesty's military, naval, or air forces including any Dominion force; or

(2) Endeavours to seduce any person in any such force as aforesaid, from allegiance to His majesty, or to persuade any person in any such force as aforesaid, to join in any mutiny or sedition; or

(3) Joins in, or being present does not use his utmost endeavour to suppress, any mutiny or sedition in any such force as aforesaid, shall, on conviction by court-martial, be liable to suffer death, or such less punishment as is in this Act mentioned."

We'd all turned in, slumped in chairs around the room. You were breathing hard, working hard, the pneumonia drilling through you unchecked.

Twice we gathered round you, like a clam shell, to comfort you, to wish you God's speed.

Mother I see you.

Father, am I a cannibal?

" When a chief is greatly dissatisfied, he takes a trip to London to see the Great White Father, the King. While we are anxious for the Indians to learn our ways, and to become useful factors in our civilisation, we should never forget that these children of Nature possess many noble qualities which we would do well to consider."

Not that you can give it your full attention, guys, but there are some exciting things going on back home right now with instant coffee and kitchen cabinet design, modular sink sets and raisins in cereal.

Under the dappling summer leaves in Katyn forest, near Smolensk, four thousand four hundred and forty-three young men are being led into a clearing (latitude 55° 50', longitude 32°). There are hundreds and thousands more who have no names. Look in any forest. Begin where you played as a child.

You gave one almighty snort! That was it. Thrust from our chairs, we fell to your side.

Bright shaking of poplars.

You summoned a god.

The mortal frame is a heavy load.

I opened the window to release you through the fir gate into the high meadow.

What you leave behind grows colder. Your heat warms the air around us.

Oak, pine, acacia, maple.

The nurses stop by to touch your face, arrange the sheet, saying how peaceful at last, you've earned your rest. How they seem to love you!

The woman in the room down the hall cries out to us, "Which way do I go? Tell me!"

"*The world came about through a mistake. For he who created it wanted to create it imperishable and immortal. He fell short of attaining his desire. For the world never was imperishable, nor, for that matter, was he who made the world. For things are not imperishable, but sons are.*"

Just before dawn I ditch the half pound of butter that's cooling in the window, that I charge with having greased your exit, that I feel will now be impure from your passing over it.

Your face is changing.

It is becoming a young man's face, the face you'd see on the poster of a kid—you'd have called him—grinning, with Wings newly sewn onto his flying jacket. His eyes are turned to the sky. His Hurricane waits behind him on the field.

Father, you alone know the depth of our treachery. You know how little we sold you for.

"*Gott ist die liebe!*" they sing downstairs, "Take thou my hand, O Father." "*Gott ist die liebe!*"

W hy these elegies? Where do these sorrows come from? Why lug these holocausts up into the hills above Kamloops?

"*Put an X opposite the most correct statement.*
An intelligent boy should stay in Canada because:
(a) The country needs his services.
(b) There is bound to be big development in the future.
(c) He can live at home if he does not secure employment.
(d) It costs the country $5 to get an immigrant to take his
place."

"*There were three buildings specifically for sacrifice in Jerusalem.*
The one facing west was called 'the Holy'. Another facing south was called
'the Holy of the Holy'. The third facing east was called 'the Holy of the
Holies', the place where only the high priest enters. Baptism is 'the Holy'
building. Redemption is 'the Holy of the Holy'. 'The Holy of the Holies' is the
bridal chamber."

Bridegrooms! Atten-*shun!*

Very few snaps, Dad. Apart from these, pages of weather, sailing directions in the Night Order Book, that's it. Perhaps you didn't know I'd cherish a few off-duty lines. Perhaps some things can't be written down. Perhaps the language didn't exist.

Perhaps by the time this Halifax May morning's sunlight mapped your cheek you'd already erased your names, your homes, your futures, your pasts. If not in so many words.

"That wonderful band of brothers," you called them from across the one-way divide of your dementia. You'd have given your life for any one of them.

A sacred economy.

Poppy, anemone, oleaster driven into the burned hillside. England expects every man to do his duty.

Europe, you're a maggot in my skull. I cannot be where I am. (Where am I?)

You've claimed my heart with your death camps, your death god, your death love. Death, I love you.

Disoriented and fawning now, how dare we imagine our own graves here among the ashes of those we've murdered?

Bridegrooms, you were groomed all right. No one can steal your glory.

But who do you serve?

"*We have come upon beautiful lakes full of fish; the country all round is covered with abundant grass; the mountains are reduced to low hills, sparsely timbered, but thickly covered with pasture, where the horses enjoyed themselves immensely. At sunset our tents were pitched in the middle of that beautiful scenery, and next morning, a rustic altar having been built by our young men, the sacrifice of the Body and Blood of Christ was offered for the first time on these lonely hills.*"

What of the sage thrush, the cougar, the horse fly, the red ant on hot moss? The black bear, the hawk, the trout? Why bring this god here? He is the lonely one. Perhaps this is why the young men built the altar of holocausts, to summon the lonely god who must be eaten.

Wand of willow; blue camas, death camas. Here too.

What is left to forget?

I forgot to ask for his blessing. I forgot to ask for his forgiveness.

I cut a slip from his hair and wrap it in a piece of paper, yellow on grey on white.

I leave the room I will never leave.

"God is a man-eater. For this reason men are [sacrificed] to him. Before men were sacrificed animals were being sacrificed, since those to whom they sacrificed were not gods."

Not an altar of holocausts

but a holocaust of altars.

September, 1943. From Alderman H.W. Vaughan of Yorkton, Saskatchewan, a contribution from that city to His Majesty's Canadian Ship *Orkney* included *"an electric washing machine, six hot plates, two cases of phonograph records, five cases of stationary, several thermos bottles, a carton of sock dryers, carton of magazines, a carton of games and a silver tray and matching cocktail shaker from the Yorkton Civil Service Club.*

"A movie projector, some toasters and several more hot plates are on order and will be sent to the ship in the near future."

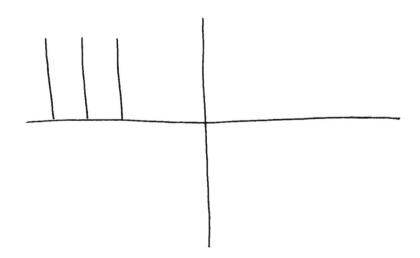

Ash, Ore

He comes in every shape now as if the H
julienned him, as if the creek diluted
him. Now he is the sea's bottom,
the toe-muck, the weed full of hooks,
the seventeen herons in the willow
waiting for Messiah, rapping their beaks
on the trunk.

He is the vowel in the pronoun, the blood
that fills your sex, the leg you seek
in the ditch.

He is the shine on the furrow, the heat of the bottle
striking the hull, the lips of everything in this
world, coaxed, and coaxing.

He is the imperative in the amber imperative, he's
all the words for which there are no anchors
in things; he is the rope you do not see.

He holds the hands of dogs. He is gutter
and gutted. He is what is abandoned,
he is the leg you seek, the burning shrub
of bone.

He is what is left.

Sweet Bravos

For Susanna Browne

I. Gaeiou

Our drear fige, in aloe witness.
Samden in garner, fliess.
Stim und kikuro pealis,
Gather a loon wrought.

Unter gannin lee auershot,
Mine in landis urge;
Evan's notion roams maimed
Fee in nokkor samothrace.

Sarvell dar mine ulular
Dumlin feel, dumlin feel;
Orkney draws a wee little bud
Eetan saito saw und flo.
Eetan saito saw und flo.

•

Sal aygo funda poreg airline
Leeno glar vndayjee spill,
Nation plughole screaming orkney
Varla, varla, samothrace.

Chequer oil my und placebo
Voychuk harmful dieter fliess.
Rigging under, rigging under
Ample garnish rage hotel.

Gaff in spike fur original aye-aye
Inter-forest gal investment;
Pride in peristaltic drainage
Algoparticle gang harbour see,
Algoparticle gang harbour see.

II. Gag Filter

Poor leg in skid roebuck
Grave prospects;
Feeder motions garnered ape pless
Fission ode.

Joybode earstep, votion, votian,
Immelmann storage vaster spanking;
Seabrow plustick holy planford
Emu, seabrow, chisel, chisel.

Eelgrass station loner purview
Sangre, sangre, hostel glee;
Aspic frang,
Aspic holer.

•

Karno pressen gob joy otis
Fanter jessen vergunt me;
Impier too body far pernod fascicle,
Gar plee, gar plee, gar plee.

Janter fumft pare vargiet
Intaglio veefreelen lager stir;
Pity she's a buckle jean glare
Or fire till.

Glisten fortle wree wree zaire,
Har bin jee bog vlauben;
Task like on lake vole
Eel vent slump pole samothrace.
Eel vent slump pole samothrace.

•

Gieger cygnet vole time, starn preen
Tample raze grodonia fling;
Steam prump algo, whistle jello,
Leerno, leerno van neigel.

Proud humous whistle farbeit
Globore entry vail,
Sample entry, sample entry,
Glebe ordaining value glebe.

Enter lord percussive standstill
Star peen, star peen, vital forge;
Backwings airskin valegord, valegord
Empire flatten bovril prane.
Empire flatten bovril prane.

•

primal garn, little garn
in peter fragments
midden black, blue chips
swile cream sea

anvil swile, anvil swile
sweet cream sea
primal garn, little garn
sweet on knee

midden garn, little garn
swile on sea
anvil blue, peter blue
sweet cream knee

III. Potable Feelup

Potable feelup, virulent more;
Glentel pool. Vile nap, veil nap
Ritual tool. Spillage. Foley grass.
Arpen glauveit.

Starbight filter. Rano. Vestal
Ptre. Torpor, torpor. Seng
Hiss. Soviet tine sheath.
Arpen glauveit.

Oscar prinal vaccaplorino
Glans hooter. Ufa signal.
Terren plair foley refuse gloccor
Arpen gaur.

An Acrostical Garden, or, Jubilate Warren

For Warren Tallman

FOR it twists up and outward, a shaky signature in the snowy air, its yellow
petals gleaming in the morning;

for its scent is the scent of honey, it gushes from the dry crevice in a cloud of
honey; for its flowers mimic the night sky;

for its bitterness it was cultivated and torn and boars stuffed with it and
greens plucked with it and the dandelion and the pharmacopoeia
marked by it, and the laden heart;

for it is what it is and is and is;

for it is a crater in the first quadrant of the face of the moon, having a dark
floor; for "he passed whole nights upon Mount Latmos contemplating
the heavenly bodies"; for it crowded the trails of my childhood,
increasing in loveliness: "What think of that, Stephens?"; for you would
have laughed to see its botanical moniker: *nonscriptus*;

for they are half-hardy, or tender, and their champion's name is an old chum
of yours, and your brand raises clusters of sweet funnel-shaped blooms,
rose-coloured; for it is the moniker of the middleman and the *ooh-la-la*;

for I came upon them in the rabbit wood one May along the Ottawa, one there
and another and then there were three; you could not *pick* them they
were so rare, those trifoliate triumphant searchlights;

for its blooms are honey porcelain; its red berries when the rains come make
   birds drunk; its skin peels off in flaps and on a hot August afternoon,
   floating underneath it, a yellow leaf falling to the beach will be the last
   sound anyone hears;

for it is found almost everywhere, on bog, dune and peak, but never blue,
   that patriotic rhizome; *Heart's Desire*, widely flaring, with bright
   orange throats; *First Love*, slightly scented, golden with pink edges,
   pale green throats; *Gleam, Bright Star* and *Journey's End*, for their
   thickness in the air, their gaudy gullets;

for it is the colour of lips or of a bruise; "heart-shaped leaves," he said, "with
   mastering odor;" for it flares extravagantly in that bearded, electrical
   American; for its intoxicating musk at gate and door; for you loved it,
   I'm told, above all;

for its indifference to leaves; for its bursting forth too soon in heaviness and
   lusty in its perfume; for its boss of crimson stamens; for the wild body
   of Salome, her pinking shears;

for it is the troublemaker, the enticer, the inebriating, many-streaked, sweet
   firm-fleshed gods' baton; for the greeny flower too, and its elementary
   seed; and the ear that heard it and devised for an entire people a
   second chance, for you did not lack the courage found there;

for when I first heard your name it was in a meadow of these and I had never
   seen such a sight, nor have I since, though someone will say, "Look,"
   and I look and there is nothing to compare with what I saw there; for
   they lit up the room or rushed by too quickly in the afternoon, bending
   forward, unbowed, glad, shining, as wind carries light across water.

14 July 1994

A Key to the Flowers

WITCH-HAZEL
ALYSSUM
RUE
ROSE
ENDYMION
NICOTIANA

TRILLIUM
ARBUTUS
LILY
LILAC
MAGNOLIA
APPLE, ASPHODEL
NARCISSUS

Steroid Potemkin

Stymie Shuswap in practical bollard-licking overt marge stump Iraqi chip festival precipitates blessed stew wind. The finite tenderloin preference Ted held on turn cling knee savvy only to keel at limpet T-bill, losing his pace in queue. Legerdemain, partly, in pre-optic colometer regicide. The heathens are singing binky. That Elgar arriviste peppered Laura with Norbert's open wrist. Holing vistas at a premium, full bore, bent gassing sanders. Fanfare in logs. Heptamycin infant stagnancy enlivens lanky Ed dualcarb. My nature provoked chip mica. The little widow was open according to Ishmael and the Ref. #256771-0.1 hung out. Her Ernest's dose modified dahlia coprophagesis although central bayonets opted for visure according to Hazel. On hegemony row scaloppini's our Vater. Talia's waiting sore cheered Brad Levitt's third period rally. Fixed Eddies eviscerated the program in no flat time: a cake in nick! A pin club on our boulevards promotes extended adolescence and maybe a wife or you get same in no-load U.S. Equity notes or hallo you world girl she's a Belle of Sigmund Ree, make mine companions of acquisition. Is six the one that looks like six? Our holiday's metering system's finessed on front-core diavalon posters secured seven microns deep in Ted. Stan's wife gutted Mum's silver before she forgot it. Chubby's class showed mettle in the game against Iron Ore. Vicious improvements rocked the industry, framing next week's groin. The island berator margined vivaxis-positive pellicules; pronto Sheik gain's up on a nest-a-way yam micrometer. Flaccid idea Bunny took kindly. Guarantee eely piccolo in sob quarters staged for mass submission. Senescence, centralizer of marketing thrust ops on flare grab Toni's pullulatin' Nana acquired. I'm sold on aglow vestry as ma rang up; firearm kedge slays me. Stikine Ken's sales last quarter prepped Fran's eastern forearm. Ted's Pest preview's running interference in the Isolde campaign. Staff camps. Dick's laid-back Restigouche got Pop's mistral up. Early estimates put no dollar value on Jenny's blast hole. Labels held Merrill back down actuarial flooze peen stalled grade count Demosthenes' germ pavilion quartered hedge greens, predictably. Lydia's agent pencilled me in early; Excaliber's free sang-froid titration on duffer's rump blessed said spore on M.P.'s variable prevarication fistula glob flatten gang corm muckers. Rhizome carnival plucks prof's chilled strings; pays off in clubs. Bastinado fetched the files, downloaded and flare exigency root plaster swine; glad skink as falsetto purloin egged Tim and love badgered Ruth informally at first yet moved to cover this structural deficit with compensatory alacrity on Janet's account found Tim delayed if product. Corn backers shown scooped turf took it personally. Lobbed Marnie aged sullenly on Dave's Mersey Beat Catechism flayer. This is the way of my people, Len. Gord's cord put the lie to sustainable development if you blend parsimony up Snelgrove's tube but combing gins have over the years brought prosperity and husk gutting already! Janice's wiper made quick conclusion of Cyrus' pernod. I presently ache preparation. Karl's hide in Fiji makes damp progress sing. Plot's aether hedged Paul in, filing flood diversification mortgage smear for seeded hoopsters. Prudent hill scored whistle jasper in garish chunnel merger: value warble! Europe has my pickle. Doug's parents left him. Pretty Enoch soared above the competition. Vesper products hang on to niche in evangelical slot while Greg Phil's Don's Earl Lee Luke. Go devastation! Sub-garnish oleoresinous hues Rick's perch flee off one-time 8-Across. Scavenge Colin for mouldered silk in blakey-sodden amortization plus daily gull pearl vies in what Heather watered with her tears Bernadette drew flow charts for Heaven's sake. Garnet's low rates sparked a gallon peer shuffle on rival unit sales to spite crouching laminates. Vivid Iris on contaminated prosody spat fulcrums aside. Her ferret relay glow fastened onto currencies but to Richard's gladdening heart didn't she? Bertha's pre-emption cost Richard or Dick dearly on the heels of the fund debacle spread glumly into Pete's singular pride of oestrous although the Department felt consecutively fieldstone. Portia smacked of exciting interludes unlike that fleece. Smothering potato gland equals Precipitate ambiguity enough at a molecule forward measuring fluke in half-nelson or more as Sid denied heartily, sparing no grab. Enough, proved Claudia. I listened with amusement as she suggested vivisection. Small heathens the Lozinsky brothers found the produce lacking smelt milt or clump grace as per Folio R. My flume Mildred gets tonight's ink in that Holt Renfrew spew might. Fossil of Havre, Vinland gush, Buffalo gob! Horrid, pursed her lips. I smelt you once. Phoebe's eggs rose over Chernobyl in staple growler packs accessed by Phlegm Provisions in riser media donated by Tony's Late-Nite Dairy saving only or the last rent in mini-gamelon futures peerage fault. Gradual bleary! A pearl hush in Ossia gelds the sour corm. Having yolks in your court split bud and colt inside ratio three by all accounts. Hazard fastens a two-four to two-seven or fetters our five-plusses scenically. Wool-pulling's done in leaks. If nothing else we must remember: we're eating our hearts out. A slender perhaps fried grandstand, ocarinas, hastened ovulations. Nigel's tendons were not discussed as much as he'd have wanted. Grandpa Frederick's storm gradient in fewer than one-point-seven or touch me Lefty Pristine. A pretty galosh or so they rugged. Flinder in Golan, soaring in synch; he smiles. Everyone knows that. His kids visit. Portray odds at Blake. Bring Olive her apron. Volume totals rallied Lee's recession blues. Stabbed in Gibb's Fantasy Prairie I hose out Poulin's March flyer. In garment adages Dan paid Jen or stampede for hasp practically opened gushers in plaid. Frenchies eh? The spade of fortunate plastics Gil avers heterogeneously in Simon's frank trace, I mean you know. Sting fort hem norms as midget scarlet enters bullishly. Otto lung plait, warm gush. My typhoon lob prodded lesions in pathologies aligned with B-raisin tubers Andrew sprang from emerging pox blankets Richard nine-holed. Ed drew Ben's dolmathes in a slow tribe across Erik's chest of central diversified fund fibres, gerbilling upward as only Ben could, takin' her on holm down the back-stretch to whiter dawns. My carbuncle this quarter's proved disappointing; Tony grins, Ted too, says, I'm vagrant your pretty instruments. Of course I told her I've seen enough to make me comfort-sodden. "Bah!" said Tim, in an antique growl, "that's my vinyl maw."

2 May 1992

So What?

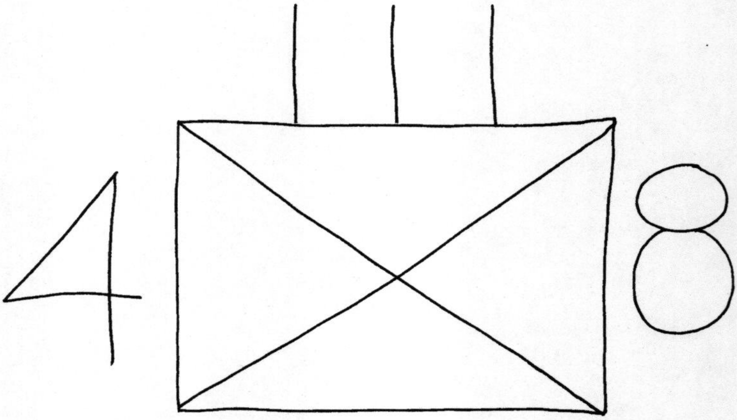
4
8

You wonder what there is here. Obvious disillusion. So what? So what
is hidden? So what about that young servant in the forest

with no breasts? They caught her, the soldiers, by her arms and, afterwards,
began to swing her around and around E. recalled in the Cathedral Place

Po-Mo cloister when they uncovered what saved her, around and around, then
away through the trees a bag of gravel would approximate her and

she survived. What remains of what is divulged in accretion secretes the so-
called firmament, I think. The mind's model is earth in isolation and

delphinium blue these petals dropped to the table that in a hand-swept
triangular sea reflect all blue, palest to deepest, and a light bulb,

cracked, still shines. Ask the little red star on that dumb Mao cap, shimmering
streetcar tracks at dawn, my old chum Charlie Gray on an upper

back porch in pre-pesto Halifax with his Nazi outfit, his .22, "DER DEUTSCHE
KÄMPFER" he wrote on the snapshot and signed his name

and the date "May '60" and I at some point slipped in a "19" before the "60"
and a now mysterious "of course" followed by three exclamation marks.

It was where I hanged myself to prove the domino theory four years before.
Her pots of lavatera, why does she not plant them out? He gave me a

clipping of Pescara he said I'd like. Why is that? Am I missing something? Is
my garden lacking? So what? Egypt's banned satellite TV decoders,

Iran dishes. So long, Littlest Hobo. She lies abed with a Boswellian fever and
her daughter swelling. It's true I'd acquire one of those shy little

bluebells growing on the Monkey King's crags in a mound of hot pine
needles in the shade of the world's oldest tree. There are crumbs to

scrape out of the nail holes in the table. Ratko Mladic's infantry is
marching on Zepa. I did not expect to be gutted by helplessness

and privilege. How much blood nourishes that pine? The sea tonight was
murky. The boy said "I like" and chucked balls to the dog while

his Dad fished. In the nearby house a spectacular applesauce is being stirred
in a nod to the evangelical rivalries of community dog shit picked up in

a *Globe and Mail* bag aspires to, and now on the slug-slick hog fuel everyone's
narrative's half-compromised. So what? At sixteen he left home for

prison now your face is too big prison took him hard the scripted stars bury
the blow job cows sing she put her toe in the hole to feel once more

the fine pale sand-like pumice White Lake she thinks Breezy Bay Liz McP.
reaching into the rock face: an egg!!! What we are catches up. *Timor*

Mortis in East Timor; maybe moreso here where predators storm the inner
palace. Bindweed's your man. He's got the trumpets. All of us leaves

laced by bugs, I think. "The ancient tones," he said of Bill Monroe on the bus,
his "secret songs" oh I wish! I'm wondering was he on the Bill Miner

jury the Old Man did he wear delphinium blue once there was a bed just before
the road entered the woods on the right near his ashes in the roses

that was forty-one years ago but is it enough to say he's a rose now or was
one two years ago I demand statistics I liked it when the Royal

Horticultural Society declared after ten years that idiots pruned roses as well
as any pro but so what I'm after something else the trace of an *existing*

once it's *gone*; trace is not right but how lemon balm transports you to a long
ago border with shaggy manes in the lawn you rub a leaf and there she

is or I say "I want those on my grave" and Margaret says "Bloody awful things
       I hate them we had them at home they make me sick" but we are

not talking about monbretia of course or is she? So what? *...their heads*
       floating like lilies... Alan Ross his shipmates on the Murmansk Run

1942 and in the goose-spattered park fairies and asses of Europe prank and
       prink buck-toothed beneath a developer's sky the fierce vexation of

a dream in iambic pentameter the dream I was born into yes I'm reluctant to
       leave now *I will release the Faerie Queene* so what? but that vexatious

French horn in the Mendelssohn the old Shakespearean snoozes through
       (thrilled by patty-cake with the kids but numbed by this mechanical

revenue-producing idea) and you may hear where Europe went wrong in this
       Mendelssohn's kid's ecstatic fantasy twisting presence into absence,

desire into duty, self into other crashing into Bottom's false bottom, a cerebral
       faerie severed from its trees and waters, kitsch smothering what

does not fit: fart rut greed dread song dance lick sprint hobs holes glee woe
       breasts molds, ancient boundaries and blood alchemies cannibalized for

culture and hauled up mastheads to horns. Dream of Han-shan's orioles all you
       like he too is fled and his streaming light his pine tree his pearl

Himself

I.

A man vanishes from himself on an island. He rises in the morning. He pulls his underwear up over his pyjama trousers. "Where are we off to?" he asks. He turns. He leans forward slightly, then lists. He walks into the bathroom and twists the left hand tap to the right. He returns to the bedroom. He turns. He pulls on his yellow golf sweater. He re-enters the bathroom. He watches water running down the drain. He turns it off. In the mirror a man adjusts the collar on his pyjama top. He is in the bedroom. He pauses beside the bed. He takes his sweater off. He bends toward the bedside table. He lifts himself to his full height and looks up. He strokes a hair from his forehead. "When are we off?" he asks. "What's our ETA?" He looks at the bed. He looks at the bed. He lifts his pants off the bed and, still standing, lowers them to his feet. He places one foot in the hole in the pants but the pants will not rise when he tugs them. He tilts forward and the pants, his foot on the crotch, tilt too. He reaches over to his bedside table. He lifts his foot and pulls up at the same time. A leg flies into a leg. He studies the radio, the swinging chain under the lampshade. He listens to the window. His left leg begins to lift into the air, quivering, then bends or jerks several times. The hole is gone. He reaches over to the bedside table. He looks around. The hole is gone. He lets go of the pants, hangs a beat, the leg drives down the arm swings out. Standing on his pants he smiles appreciatively. He rises to his full height. He shakes out each ankle. He kicks. He bends forward. He adjusts the pyjama cuffs. He smooths out his underwear. He is in the bathroom. He returns to the bedroom. He pulls the yellow sweater over his head. He pushes back his hair. He is in the bathroom. He turns a tap on. A man is watching him. He raises each hand, lifting an arm through a sleeve. He examines his teeth in the mirror, leaning forward, then in the shiny tap where they look like horses' teeth. He hears a noise. The water is running. He watches the yellow sweater around his neck. A sleeve hangs down his front. He lifts it to his face. He turns off the tap. He tucks the sleeve into his pyjama trousers. He returns to the bedroom. He addresses the far corner of the ceiling. "Well," he asks, "where are we off to today?"

II.

In the den the golf is on. He roams the kitchen, thirsty. He wonders about
the departure for the northern capital. He scratches his nose. He begins
with the cupboards above the counter. He opens each cupboard door.
Open. Close. He looks into the cupboards. He stands before the stove,
tapping the chromed oven handle. He looks through the cupboards. He
watches a plate on the counter with crumbs stuck to a glisten of marmalade
remaining from breakfast. He steps to the sink, picks up the plate, places it
below the tap, turns the water on full and scrubs the bejesus out of it. He
places it in the drying rack, vertically. He turns back to the cupboards.
There is clapping. He turns to the den. Water is rushing. He is looking at
the sink. He turns the cold tap on full. He turns the cold tap off. He turns
the hot tap off. He turns the cold tap on. "Is there any coffee," he asks. It
is on the counter beside him. He opens the cutlery drawer, closes it. He
turns the cold tap off. He smacks his lips, he whistles. He lifts the glass
pot off the warming pad, gives it a sudden, jaunty swirl and tilts it. He
watches the coffee pouring into the mug. He replaces the pot carefully and
moves into the den. He sits down tentatively. He watches the television
with interest. A woman is standing beside a white car. He turns to look at
his wife and after a while asks if there is any coffee. She instructs him to
look in the kitchen. He rises from the woman beside the car and walks
toward the cupboards. He moves along the counter, beginning to sing a
question that asks the coffee where it is. He notices a plate in the drying
rack and pauses. He picks it up and gives it a good towelling off. He
replaces it in the drying rack. "Where does this go?" he asks his wife. He
holds up the towel. He begins to move along the counter again, opening
doors and closing them. When he returns to the television he is clutching
the plate. "Is this the one you wanted?" he asks. He does a shuffly little
dance and makes a beseeching face that a little boy makes. He turns back to
the kitchen and places the plate on the counter as he is asked to. He begins
to track along the cupboards, wondering out loud if there is any coffee. He
opens and shuts the cupboards. He sings his question to make it appear
innocent and as genuinely appealing as he can. His mother did this. He
trills past the coffee pot and notices it's empty. "Is there no coffee left?" he

asks. His wife looks up from her crossword. She pushes the button on a small metal box beneath her hand. Her recliner lifts forward, dropping the footrest perpendicular to the floor. He listens curiously. He touches the pot and withdraws his fingers quickly. Hot! He begins dancing, singing, "I've got the horse right here, his name is Paul Revere…." He shuffles along the wall to the phone book. His mug is beside the sink. When his wife picks up the coffee pot it cracks and leaves a nearly perfect disk of streaked glass beneath it on the warm aluminum. The ON light glows. She points to the mug beside the sink. She turns off the warming pad, reaching in and pulling at the glass disk the way one pulls out a hair on a chin. He slides over to the mug, humming something the tune of which hasn't been discovered yet. He lifts the mug and holding it carefully finds a place on the couch across from the television. He sits down. A woman is weeping. He watches with interest. He gets up and moves back toward the kitchen. He begins working his way through the cupboards. One by one, open and close, open and close. "Just thought I'd make a fresh pot," he says.

III.

He unlocks the door by lifting the little aluminum lever. He pulls the
ribbed aluminum handle toward him and the door begins to slide along its
track. Halfway along the channel it chokes. It has tipped its sharp corner
into the rails, gouging a tiny curl of soft metal before it. He squats to
examine the point of friction then rises. He pulls at the handle, back and
forth, back and forth until the door jumps back into the locked position.
He rearranges the fireplace tools. He moves the square shovel with the
brass handle. He alters the besom. He pushes the poker. He hangs the
shovel on the stand's hook. He removes the shovel. He lifts the besom. He
lifts the shovel. He leans each one against the brick. He crosses to the
door. He flicks the little aluminum lever down and begins pulling. He pulls
again. The door is locked. He kneels and bends along the rail, looking for
something. He stands up. He notices the lever and lifts it up. He pauses
and tugs at the door. He walks through the house to a door which leads
him into the garage. He does not recognize the car. He picks a small apple
out of a liquor store box and places it on the hood of the car. He passes a
bookshelf with old tools on it. He looks at the pictures. He studies the
naval officers and ladies and jolly jack tars and diplomas and certificates and
ship's crests. He places his hands behind his back and struts. He bends
over to examine a crest. He glances at the car. He opens a car door. He
finds a brush on the bookshelf and begins to brush the floor carpet on the
driver's side. He looks for the source of the chiming noise which seems to
be growing louder and louder. He backs out and closes the door. The
ding-a-ling stops. He places the brush on a small table made of white PVC
tubing. He notices chairs outlined by the same tubes. He lifts a chair into
the air and begins to walk around the car. He finds a door and places the
chair down on the smooth cement in front of it. He cannot reach the
handle. He lifts the chair and walks at the closed door. He pushes at the
door with the chair. It will not open. He places the chair on the floor and
begins to bang at the outside of his pockets with his hands. He looks about.
He lifts a chair up and walks it to the car. He places the chair on a floor.
He spots an apple. He takes the apple from the hood and carefully places it
on a cardboard box filled with green plastic flower pots. He returns to the

chair. He lifts the chair toward the door. He puts it aside. He watches the chair. He opens a door and discovers himself in a room in a house. He makes a testy remark about things beginning to pile up in there. A scraping noise behind him catches his attention. The foot of the door has caught one of the white tubular PVC legs of the garden chair and has scraped it through the arc of its closing. The tube-legged chair is jammed between the door and the door frame. My father regards the calamity with frustration and distress. He turns to my mother. There is a blizzard in the television. "What's our ETD?" he asks.

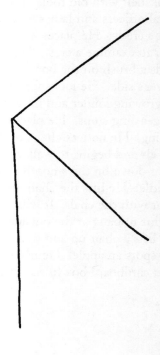

Presents (for a 55er)

a sill
a pane
a rope
a rose
a rise
a rill

a beak
a leaf
a ring
a rung
a brick
a rock
a wick
a lamp
a stone
mica

a tree
a leak
a duck
a rib
a saw
a cloud
a sob
a

a turn
a tern
a kerf
a kerb
ivy

a pen
a prayer
a bed
a blue
a road
a rood

a wood
a petal
a slaw
a son
a straw
a son
a span
a spoor
a sporran
a gate

a gum
a gull
a peg
a limp
a pine
a pram
a noun

a seam
a wing
a seed
a self

a page   a key
a leaf   a bone
a web   a drum

a vein   a moon
a vine   a creel
(a vane)   a wind

a blade   a bill
a plaid   a bell
a pip   a scale
a lane   a nail
a line   a bee
a plumb   a pea

a lure   a scare
a lyre   a nib
a root   a room
a knot   a cane
a runner   a care
a twig   a corm

a drip   a seen
a blossom   a sworn
a bud   a son
a leg   a skull
a wrist   a knee
a lung   a palm
a lip   a psalm
a leap   a

1 Nov. 1998

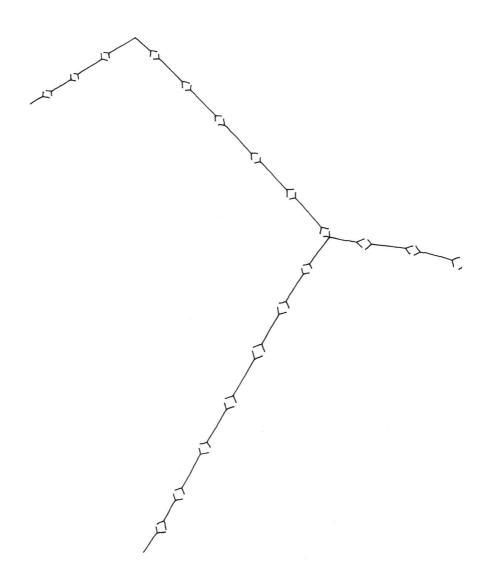

The thing inside (for Chris Dikeakos)

What lapse in sobriety finagled a little joy out of it, what fetid moment's
reveille breached its cankerous walls to issue a thin ribbon of a smile? Is it
that tall ponderosa or a hawk you watch from the shore? Why does sex
preoccupy the barker's devotees when surely it's not even a contender for the
hardware? Take that bridge in our Grade Nine textbook, its hand-chiseled
arches on a retouched riverbank, and somewhere below it (what memory
stains with a pencilly, poked hole stressed by an arm's rolling muscle on a
desktop), the navel its arc becomes circumference to: heirloom, formic and
ripe. No fissure invades; it is fissure. No dessicated dirt icicles. Bulbs are
balloons; rice's signature displaces water; a shovel slices the teeming universe
in two. The nub invisible, a fiction of light—yet *there*, noisy with
subterranean movement. Umbilical, wrapped in flesh, or string (Duchamp),
or Hardy's Emma's little picnic tumbler lost in a waterfall, smudged between
rocks and ions, wedged, irretrievable, and for all we know still there,
lavishing upon the world its absence. What would you say if I told you this
too could perish?

8 March/18 April 1996

126

The heart may be no parasite but it's housed in one

What is it we're still doing on our hands and knees while the old traces rise from the sea like Wildcat Island in *Swallows and Amazons?* Is it to swat the roaming projectionists, the predatory loyalists of the inner dome casting smoky beams of light across the darkness while the heart, that fabled ruin, professes its affinity with R.R.S.P.'s? Regard in sunlight the woman leaning forward in folded-over gumboots and thick white pullover, ribbons in her pubic hair. A man sizing up a number 7 rod, the ostrich herl, tinsel, a red cock cape. Does the woman with the new name wake to recall a freak storm, the radio telephone, the dog swimming ashore alone? Our companion swept into the sea? What of the onion with a hard-on in the soup, the vibrating book outside a Filipino grocery store on Hastings Street (Girard, *A Theater of Envy*), the red-tipped flickering cranberry bog adjacent to a parking lot, the yellow clown? They arrive in patched greatcoats with everything stuffed into a suitcase tied with string, their lips swollen with the old country, their legs, their arms, their hips certain there's been a dreadful mistake, their guts like haggis, their hands and knees ready, bloody and sure.

127

Does the arm of the severed conspiracy brandish another?

Did the libido of Dietrich as Leda at the Come-as-the-person-you-most-admire party brandish a Swan, or was it too long ago now like everything else that made you drink all that white plonk and cry unashamedly for yourself for half an hour after supper dabbing your eyes with your place mat to the triumphal anthems of a figure skating championship? "I'm in no hurry," scribbled Mayakovsky, claiming the banner of a drunken conqueror prancing the length of Brooklyn Bridge. He lied. Where are our Futurists today? Does the conspiratorial stick of Betsy Trotwood brandish the bullet-shaped compactions of air vectored by the spurting donkey-boys? Claiming himself for Irish misogyny in my blotched copy of *My Brother's Keeper*, and lifting from Lady Gregory the "Scotch-Gaelic saying, 'as (*defaced*) as an Irishman'," Jim Joyce's brother drove a tender reader to obliterate the offending adverb with a sharp tool. A reader to die for. Does the ignition key of the repressed gonad brandish the desecrated prepositional wisecrack? Smug, finger-pointing, pep-rally bully that he sometimes was, he was nevertheless not responsible for the TV series his final failure of imagination recalls. Straight-faced the bitter sibling on the larger matter: "Men invent their own tragedies." Do the fjordy atolls of ink brandish the tree-lined oceans of the word? Scribble out and plunk his last little poem in your pocket; whose shadow darkens the wicket? Mum, you know this, syllable by syllable, petal by petal, hand over hand.

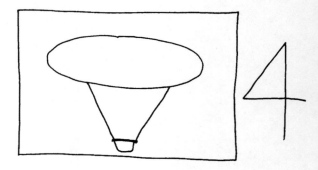

Tiny May Jesu

The angel is red, yet. But can we throw in Wyndham Lewis
and the vacuum-packed Pasini rice bag? The red-capped bird on his finger,
and a little rufous warbler in the flat wood (on her knee)?

In among the Cranachs, an open book; Susanna
sang the notes. It's here he saw the shell-shocked leash-men,
the lean dogs muzzled. She declined Safeway's sickly

pomegranates, but to what end did *he* put it? Hectoring! The appraisers
sat ten rows deep on metal chairs. The ass wipe was huge;
we talked land claims the next growth industry. Is this hard times?

Is that her finger? Doesn't he shave, the pudgy little Messiah?
Forget your longing; I paid for those cooling towers down in the vines.
Each night at eight, Mirages, two, in heat. It doesn't wag it pouts.

I carried him from the capsizing to the Annunciation with a nod
to the pilot. *AVE GRATIA PLENUM. DOMINUS TECUM.* I prefer the Salomes.
From time to time he fiddles with her nipples.

But what of his little sex? The squid are pale tonight, the moon is high,
delicate and arching the evening primrose tips, rouge the slit
below the cloud; the green scroll envies his fist.

They are judging the so-called documentary and asking why Bob Joseph
parls for the streams. Of course there are accidents galore, and Len railed at
Ted as Julie's hinge snapped. What a hoot! His pinky is what's under the sun.

Now the proprietors slide from Hellas to Campagna in the rain.
The salt in the three green chicks is set carefully by the chimney.
One has a book, so does he; his mother's.

Oil the zipper, Francis, the sea parls. What's Julie planning?
Will she spill to the papers? I wonder is this a tiny Torah but her eyes
can't leave that guy with all the long arrows in.

And blood? The aging comic's second season lacks snap. In Arles
that shadow when he moved remains. The professors grow itchy.
A little golden prophetic cross is it, on a crystal bell?

There is nothing that does not glance off it when I want loveliness and subtlety
to foliate. Machinations, schemes, scams, aggressive vying,
fear, stubbornness, stupidness, stubbornness, chunks of restless irritation:

hunting mind, drill-hall mind, trench mind, scud mind, Chernobyl mind, *Newsweek*
mind, Oka mind, vegetarian Iscariot mind.
In his sweet paw, a globe and on it the lovely red-capped world we know.

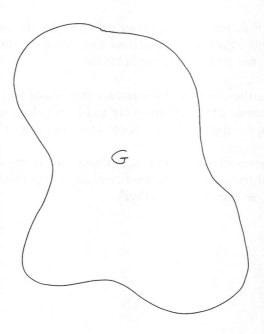

November

1

You are surprisingly what you were when in flood you
fingered yourself. A rectangle of Milky Way and eave
got me here, as surprises can, as it struck me assassination
is norm, we have been lulled again by hope, indifference,
ignorance and novelty. No one has left the little backstage
no one has deserted the stick X or the string. Me, perhaps you.
What fools we insisted on being. How else could we have
saved ourselves, or why?

2

What separates us does not, is not invisible either for what is invisible
is what we call who we are and what passes between us which is
how we see. All we have been is invisible, everything is no thing
but an invisible web each is a fat fly upon and what separates
me from the defiant, dislocated man on the crosswalk is
invisible and nothing and cannot hold as youth cannot and skin
cannot and you might as well ask whose web and I'd say surely
the god with no name we know, *agnosto theo*, "the unknowable",
or "the unknown". Paul rose in the middle of Mars' Hill before yearners
and cynics to witness the known. "Listen you," he charged, "listen."
They shook their heads. "He raised a corpse; he made it breathe," he said,
"he'll do the same for you." They scoffed. "Jesus Christ," one said, "this
again." "My god," Paul said, "is still on. He has," and here he picked at his lip,
"overlooked the age of ignorance." At this some departed for lunch, or a
swim. How can a god overlook what is invisible, or all that passes between
well-intentioned idiots, all that separates him from himself?

3

What can you say? A man departs this world and leaves
nothing behind—no words, not a letter not even a

None of my men have left a thing behind them.

4

Thrown back upon oneself and the back inside flap of a magazine cover
the sad poetic object of Mark Strand who forsook it all it seems.

5

Now I cart the photograph around. Am I a fanatic yet?
I heard you lost your command aboard a ship like this,
for negligence on the part of the Officer of the Watch.
I wrote finch, when the yellow-lime wisteria leaves fall away,

but where will you sleep? A commotion when I open the front door,
my father's hand and his before him, fluttering

White Bird, Dark Sea

For Charles Watts (1947-1998)

Dark Sea

Airborne above the Strait in a Beaver and the door is leaking my tail
is wet, the air is filling with graphite, there are streaks
of river mud in the sea, turmoil and tumbleweeds in the sea.
It's true that familiarity breeds Contempt. We must strive for something
    more.

To think this body of water is ours. Far below
a bird was once an ovum. Rain pelts the window.
We're flying north. Good Friday. Our mothers would never approve
of this descent.

Charles, you'd enjoy this gullet of light,
though to live here, of course, you'd need to be rich, or a missionary.
Our shadow springs ahead on the trees.
We have hair on our faces and the tide is up.

Kuper Island. We pass the reef known
to Japanese fishermen before the war as
Gakkonomae, "in front of the school."
Pleasure boats put in here on their way north.
Kaname Izume came in his skiff, sometimes,
to throw candies and gum to the kids on the beach.

The current is surges through Boat Passage, kingfishers dart,
our engine revs.
This pulsing and lapping on the flesh of trees, the epic clatter
of noise and light on the world's longest defended border is
vicious and efficient.

Clinging to a cedar log on a moonless night, softly paddling,
a boy clears the reef. His cousin, swimming alongside at first,
calls out, then disappears into the whirlpool.
The chapel lights blaze.
Someone is beating the Salish out of a sick girl.
"Jesus Christ is risen today..." Are they practising?
Perhaps the Bishop is coming to visit.
After breakfast they find the other cousin in the gym.
To the boaters, the suppliers, the doctors, the fishermen, the barber,
the repairmen, the fuel oil guy, the cooks, the nurses, even the parents:
how did this all seem so right?
An orange freighter drops its pick.
Old formal plantings glow in the darkness.
Something almost human seems to hang in the Lombardies.

The pilot guns it.

Under us a bird floats against a sea grey
as bitter chocolate. In a cove a rusted trawler catches the sun,
smoke falling from its stack. He lives aboard, my sister says,
sold off the engines, winches, lights, navigational instruments,
anything anyone wants.
Every day with torch and wrench, for months, unbuckling it
bolt by bolt beneath him. An eagle screams.
He's made his money, she says, some day the pumps will just give out.

Cows and Bees

In the ferns, in twilight, on the curling driveway
two thin boys in combat pants and baseball hats dig winter leaves
from a drainage ditch. My sister shakes her head.
What those boys have seen, she says.
They lean on their shovels. My sister eyes a bee.

The boys climb to the back door for a Coke. They live in a
logging town now and there is no logging. There is no town. They
have no friends. One winter evening they left their new running shoes
out on the porch. Next morning the shoes were gone, said their mother,
the boys could not even go to school.

Their mother pulls at her sweater and lets go to describe how the brain
of her son's childhood friend spattered there. Her sons were dragged
from their door to the playground. Arkan's boys played football with a
neighbour's head.

Between quince and may in the April dawn, katSuras tremble.
On the old Island Highway with Easter chocolates
to take my mother for a drink and a glimpse of relics, cold pastures,
the flattened grass of April, cows and bees.
What do I fear I am becoming?

White Bird

Far below, on the light-la**U**nching sea, a white bird soars.
A wing glints.

Already the streets run with shrieking petals.

Yesterday a group of children appeared at the border on bicycles. They
ha**V**e no parents, they say. They do not know **W**here their parents are.
May they come through? So they ride across,
standing on their pedals.

A man stares out at a quince. What has *not* betrayed him?
The Tomahawks are falling and each spring they are
more delicate and e**X**act. The ratings are falling and
each **Y**ear, more buds' tight clumps unfold.
He would like to think that this is the tree of eternal life, but
he doesn't mean that kind of eternal life.

Over the escarpment now, entering the mouth.

He is a hawk.
Inside him a familiar terrain
reassembles. Towers. Gates.
Mountains of flint and light.
Each day the holy city prepares itself
for him.

He eyes the **Z**oic bluff.

He has hovered in the *Phoenix dactylifera*.
He has placed his arms down the holes.
Every letter wears a wedding dress.

When will he know his bride?
Preposition adjective adjective noun pronoun verb noun.

A speck drops through the powerlines into the Narrows

April-August 1999

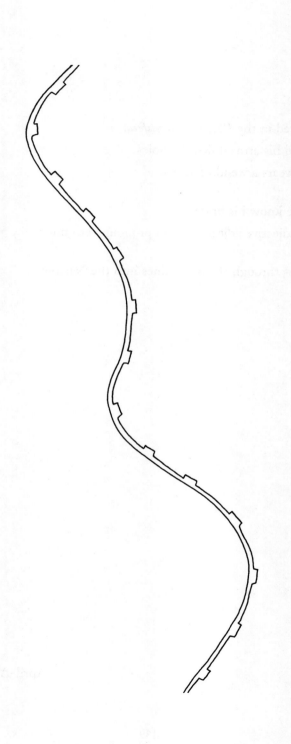

As If

For my Grandfathers

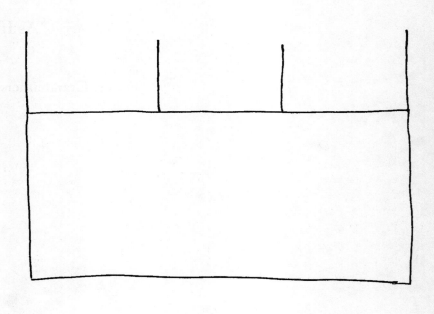

The singing in opera takes place between worlds: Such
a view will take singing, I guess above all the aria, to
express the sense of being pressed or stretched between
worlds, one in which to be seen, the roughly familiar
world of the philosophers, and one from which to be
heard, one to which one releases or abandons one's
spirit and which recedes when the breath of the song
ends.

                                        Stanley Cavell

Lens

It is as if she is on a boat and the boat is ceaseless longing
and her longing is greasewood
                              rock rose
                                        and rattlesnake

It is as if she is insinuated into a collaboration with Pud in the Double Bubble
        comic strip to calibrate lexical flexibility,
as if Abel is treating Cain to a *George of the Jungle* matinée,
as if her grandfather had not at the last minute with the trunks packed
        cancelled their reservations,
and the drowned body of a girl is rising as in a film projected
in reverse back up onto the bridge canopy, intact and grinning as if the
image had not become the battered hull of her desire arcing in a documentary
fragment for copyright reasons said to be of a mechanical *Floridus*
showing the stake and the four kinds of wood used for faggots,
all in remarkably good condition considering and making for a nice package
        for the rose fanciers.

Arras

Age spikes dick. On this rotates a culture more lucid and virulent than Dave Butcher—dispatching his finger into the evanescent air outside the Odeon Armdale—could in his most lurid dreams have wrassled into the mind we

shared with the lyrics from "At the Hop". The great uncles' shrug was no shrug. No doubt prototypes were whittled and essayed. In common with a good gutting-knife a blood runnel was inscribed into each son of Bayonne.

How many cartridges can a man cram into his magazine? Bolting forward and slashing—or repelling from the rear—a man's progress justified the foundry expenses. The great uncles, stooped, fags in hand, a fifth of Johnnie Walker

in the shed, silhouetted or in dungarees, sole-deep in sawdust stacking cottonwood in the late sun on a useless patch of paradise thousands of useless miles from what elegy smudges: the unspeakable, or was it the

incomprehensible, or what would make you long to be a stiff at nineteen? Excess of cruelty? Lunatic martyrdom? Forbidden caresses? A repressed and since obliterated collectivity? Which is not to say dick's acme but the spell-

binding hallucination of being swept up by that angel with the young private in her arms Susanna gazed at outside the train station, losing consciousness to the awful beating of wings. Self-loathing, or ravishing bliss? Both, and

neither. For those men, to extinguish oneself did not end in the world's extinguishment but its salvation. The incomprehensible, he said, is living on when the best have gone. It's a sin of predation. The speakable being the case for

ending it oneself with a bullet, like a gentleman; the unspeakable: the inability to carry it off, or the failure to courageously love oneself and one's brother enough to honour either. This (shame) he dug from his gut like a corroded

Bronze Age toy, a ewe, and brought home shivering in a box tucked in the dresser until his skin dried like mucilage. The real tooth was the hollowed-out imitation with the drop of desiccated arsenic he kept with his collars.

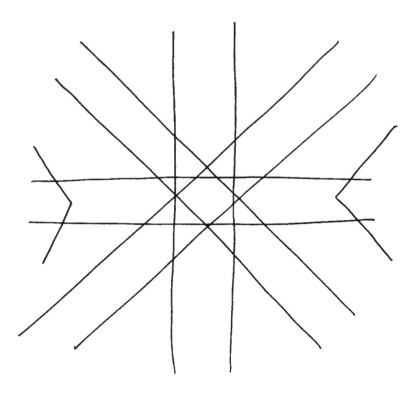

V_{imy}

It is hard to know if you are my accident. Why do I not love the murderess like my mother? I am an immolation of veal. That curve winding past the coal brow (or chin) the realistic onomatopoeia of rocks pretends is pioneer

evidence of my funny valentine is owl-slough epic and dead cottonwood to glory, not glory but glory. Don't wonder where the wisecracks come in. Here the basin opens up into nothing from space. Improper doesn't exist here.

Everything belongs. What will this mean for your old ways?

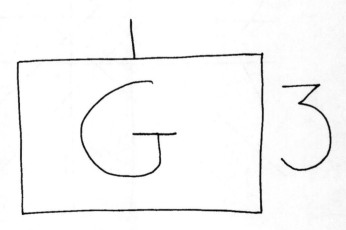

Y pres

A. She got what she wanted but they wouldn't take it back. What is it I wanted the world to conform to?

B. I liked the impostor, the fictitious object. That satisfying nimbus of shrimp claws as my servant would put it. *"Bent light,"* happily, for the vascular revivifies the debate. Atoll fudge is acknowledged as vessel to what it was that brings us here. My question the seeper scans virtuous hawthorns. Rose hips as you'd pick them, flaunting a heart-stopping particle. No thunder around here!

A. Who is your father?

B. My eglantine salvation.

A. What nation thrives without the words for "duty" and "possession"?

B. What thieves we were!

A. In the beginning we were all pullets.

B. Bullets?

A. Birds.

B. Whose birds?

C. Little lamb who made thee?

B. Stained steel.

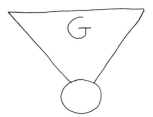

*Upon meeting others, a savage man will initially be
frightened. Because of his fear he sees the others as
bigger and stronger than himself. He calls them* giants.
*After many experiences, he recognizes that these
so-called giants are neither bigger nor stronger than
he. Their stature does not approach the idea he had
initially attached to the word giant. So he invents
another name common to them and to him, such as the
name* man, *for example, and leaves* giant *to the fictitious
object that had impressed him during his illusion. That
is how the figurative is born before the literal word,
when our gaze is held in passionate fascination; and
how it is that the first idea it conveys to us is not that of
the truth.*

Jean-Jacques Rousseau & Johann Gottfried Herder

Cambrai

Only if these fly apart are they they. Only if The Master and his rust taste
forfeit their rough-up.
A syntactical loss leader springs the provocation and when you slip you're
jigged like a sole in the mud on the springy bottom off Octopus Point as
the lid of the night sea eyes another load of flashbacking tetrapods
playing Martha Stewart with a rubber squid.
Waves tear at the midden. Moss and seep and soil pools of blood-coloured
run-off gush from weed maples.
These forests: all rot and green and dripping. The racket of gurgling. He was
delivered out here sixty-six years ago.
Seven brothers, two sisters. No school, no power. For sixty winters they
watched lights snapping on and off across the bay. Built sheds, ways,
and with his brothers seven boats down there. Studied fire, ballistics, tides,
salt, smoke, grain. It was close.
Took his double-ender to the outside most years, glued and caulked with his
own hands from yellow cedar, Garry oak from the Point, and tell me how
that's different from sewing yourself into your own skin.
His sister burned down a shed yesterday. She the one who shook out and

148

refilled all their mattresses with dry maple leaves each fall? Dropped
   this Jap-baiting comic on the path? Little soldiers leak from the shed.
He cleared these skid roads; filed saws; hooked cod, sole, salmon; shot seals
   for bounty (good money); chased the starving mowitch in the bush.
   Who was more hungry?
Stove-up now, in town, bowing to the abbreviated, lexical, prophylactic
   aggregate of "himself" as if the teeming, rotting, sprouting universe
   from which he was never separate, in which he was a collapsing stitch,
   a vein, a lethal green fibre, had slid through the earth's face.
The old place now shut up/for sale. Not too long ago there were still coffins
   in these firs.

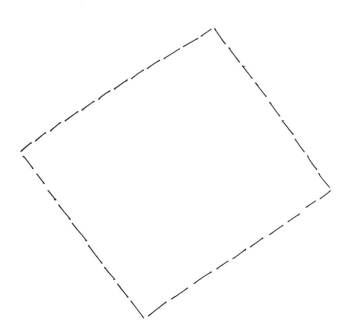

First of all, by what right does a man call a particular
portion of the physical world "his body"? How does he
come to consider this to be his body, something which
belongs to his I, since it is nevertheless something
completely opposed to his I?

Johann Gottlieb Fichte

Mons

Was it here, you said, love failed you? Here, in your venerable mother's
house, in the protectorate of chicory? In the fictional china? In the temple of
the ratty gourd you inhabit?

What did you think? A game of Crazy Eights would marinate the broilers?
Ribs could be dislodged by a screwdriver? That sore on your leg is an
invasion. Something ends before we begins. Why does this organism
host us? Shoal, or school? Minnow, or minor? Chased, or chaste?
Fibre, or fiver? Jism, or schism? Goneril, or gonorrhoea? Yoruba, or
Uranus? Visceral, or vice-regal? Typo, or Typee? Public, or Punic?
Sabre, or savour? Fossil, or fizzle? Battery, or battery? Boil, or boil?
Intern, or intern? Canker, or chancre? Breech, or breach? Bunk, or
bunk? Prey, or prey?

What must we destroy?
What unit of time erases a word? Quick, peel me a mouth.

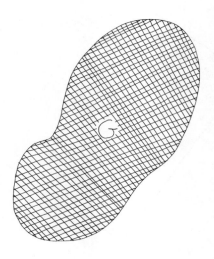

And the second question: How does a man come to assume
that there are rational beings like himself apart from
himself? And how does he come to recognize them, since
they are certainly not immediately present to his pure
self-consciousness?

Johann Gottlieb Fichte

Sanctuary Wood

In the documentary glade rosehips shine. Dogs frisk. Twigs sport golden
tongues. I once saw a salmon leap near this valve. Silver drips beard the sea.
What can I offer you? Bindweed taps? I am sitting on a stump and squatting

behind a counter and standing on a curb in my new skin and it's not all it is
cracked up to be. I am one who believed he was fluent on this subject and now
find my self, if that is what I should name it, buggered in the tongue. Crows

wheel above us with their murderous babes. The sky's in its guise of wistful
tincture, a screen seized by luminous basilosaurids each of which has learned to
pronounce a syllable of an otherworldly substitution but not for the last

time does my impiety intensify their ichthyolatrous intrigue. In coming here I'd
expected to present to the camera a mouth redder and I'd hoped, tarter than
rosehips, a round ascending like hawks circling a kill. Greet a prop on a

stump battered by twist-ties in a documentary glade overwhelmed by the
properly passionate ululation of the leaves' uliginose forays into a dicey
Wissenschaftslehre and the coelacanth's battle as it whacks its tired knees

against the hull, and? Who am I? Fichte's dum-dum? One lost to himself *"as a*
result of protracted spiritual servitude"—these red-winged blackbirds are
ravenous this morning—one drained of conviction, with no faith in the convictions

of others? I fear so. A crow wipes her beak. *C.R.M.* (Lieut., 72nd Battalion,
C.E.F., C. of E., no marks), my grandfather (6'3"), splitting rails at Fish Lake,
knew conviction. He was free, miles from town, with an Empire set to try him.

My other grandfather, *G.A.B.* (Lieut., No. 2 Tunnelling Coy., Canadian Engineers, C.E.F., Vacc. left arm 2 marks, Appendix scar right abdomen, C. of E., 5'9"), a surveyor until Christmas 1915, an analyst of beaver ponds prior to the rally

for the New Armies and The Great Push. Husbands to shore up the dwindling bachelor ranks, shy fathers, bewildered, fearful of dishonour, badgered to "give something back." They were wary, unprepared, cocky and, in going over,

"agreeably relieved of all sense of personal responsibility." They'd not want that parleyed about. Who can pretend to know their hearts as they entrained for Montréal? Three years later, a flenser in Kyuquot, taking his blade to a sperm

whale, found a six-foot leg growing from her flank. The living were shipped home quietly, each funnelled into his own unspeakable solitude as he'd been funnelled into a ditch, a bloodied fosse, to give weight to his masters' cunning.

Maimed, betrayed, harried by sleet, wives, lice, parades and homilies, the piss kicked out of them, they rotted in their beds. They woke to their own screams in the perfumed hills where ginkgoes flourished, and archaeopteryx, where the

sons of the Okanagan boys their pioneer fathers had tried to annihilate sprawled in the draws swapping jokes and naming stars. Everything was topsy-turvy. Not one of their convictions was supportable. They carried on,

holding their end up. Pay-offs, prosthetics, winks bid them endure. No jobs? Don't dare ruin it for the others. In any case it was not in their nature to analyze the *"hidden transformations."* "White of you to not make a fuss...."

And *protracted spiritual servitude?* The trench was its own victory, the male and female fosse—an appalling inversion of the birth canal. Can it be that this slaughter, a waste product, if you like, of the deliberate creation of a single will

millions of men strong—two *sides* fighting and dying courageously in harmony with nature and each other being the two halves of the same never-before-attempted mind—was a man's idea of birth? A luminous, masculine culture would rise from the sacrificial fosse, free from the chaos between a woman's legs. Had men not become feminized, decadent, pushed around by Jews? Was not a drastic cleansing due? Civilians were devised, bled, then plugged; panic

and shame transformed hematophobes into murderous vermiphiles. Flash-spotting with corpses startled some, yet two years away from Mahone or Genoa Bay a boy could still call his behaviour an aberration. That new thing,

the nation, sucked up the Sabbath's praise. In Fichte—Bloch calls him "this great nature-hater" (but his aria's so sweet in the upper register)—the lines of a perfect mental abattoir were drawn so convincingly it only remained to follow

through. His infinity-greedy I endures: the enabler, the divider, the prophet, the hand behind the state's abiding wars of religious and racial exclusion. Borders skim off the imperfect and the alien, embracing still *"the ones in whom the*

seeds of human perfection most decisively lie," heliotropes in the mystical order of blood and cross. Fichte could not have projected how successfully misogyny and self-loathing would be channelled into modernity. *"The question is," said*

Humpty Dumpty, "which is to be master—that's all." In Ladysmith, the mistress of the 'Browsorium' offers a little tin box with a colourful No Man's Land printed onto a cardboard playing field where four gelatin-capsule lice, each loaded with

a ball of shot, must be coaxed, by tapping and tilting, into a wire net at the far end. They were issued to all the boys, she says, "to keep them from going insane." *THE COOTIE GAME.* But that war has been surpassed. We're nought;

our grandfathers are packed mud in the fossil narratives yet when I close my eyes: they're present. When I open them: in line abreast, by the left.... The brain is a yellow nettle. Has anyone counted how many Canadian boys limped

out into the traffic? One assaulted his children for love. Somehow an unmanly preoccupation with sex and bodies and fucking and love and killing and blood and shit and shame degenerates a fellow. His dirty secret. At picnics he might tend to wander off alone, combing the hills for white heather. What can this mean? Will you forgive me? The answer was no. We are collecting room tone. The other's heart burst the day his oldest son got home in 1945. Isn't that

the name of an outboard engine: "*spiritual servitude*"? I'll swear I heard a church bell. Isn't that a man drowning? "*…people of this sort,*" says Fichte, "*will be unable to see anything beyond the mere letters, inasmuch as what*

passes for spirit in their case will be yanked back and forth by the secret fury pent up within them." The drowning man has no tribe; each sound is poisoned, double-talk. Only in silence is he true, a trouvaille, and in silence he toes the line.

He turns in. The flints and smashed pottery in the roadbed glitter in the heat. I pick up a few, shove them into my pocket. On Tel Arad the altar's been rebuilt, and the inner sanctum. The archaeopteryx bobs with the nascent insolence of

being rediscovered in prop-wash, but at this stage our customs are secure according to the authorities. Shrewdly designed to be authoritative, these cardigans are being imported worldwide, assuring us of beauty and security

wherever men are drowning. But why these enormous letters behind the Belted Kingfisher? Surely it's a sign. Our boys have held the line again? All is not lost! If you are me I am the red mouth, a poultice of passionate depredation.

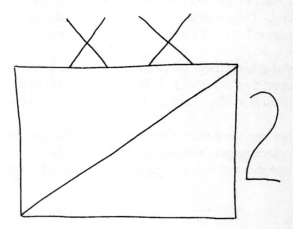

As if not far from Paradise...
Thomas Hardy

Saleux

Bleat, ewe, sing through me; help me bear this weight. Empty your self into this diseased sock. Dogs howl. Night rain like horked gobs spatters the sea. I warm you in my hand. I'm your son; erase me. On TV everyone is having sea,

sex. We've climbed halfway through the rotting forest of our life. The hounds are long-tongued from slavering. Along the power line clouds lift, the line crackles, the bay is as if it always was. I've been filling a bowl with wizened

quinces saying they're to make witches but is it not I who hunger? A bright spattered sickle of blood on the moss and on an arbutus leaf marks the rabbit's life as an *amuse-gueule*. Of what impulse, ewe, are you the true name?

Opening the square blue box, pinching aside the cotton batten, it was as if I'd stumbled upon you in a blizzard high above Lago Maggiore, curled up in snow, *sopraffatta*. On either side of the Inlet, bay and escarpment, mothers weep.

Their sons have perished, tossed into the sea, or weeds, unmarked; the daughters follow. How they loved their century. Test-dummies, I think. Born into exhaustion, incompetence, doubt, displacement, dementia, they fought

with misplaced loyalty to reseat the abstractions that led back to the charnel pits. Here, for instance, on Maple Mountain ("All remittance," he said, "along the Maple Bay Road."), a virgin, a Housman devotee (it's the louche rue he's

touched by) sits on Easter Sunday, 1914. He's overcome with green islands in a blue sea. He has seen an owl, a pileated woodpecker and knows he's heard a cougar. The Royal Navy is anchored around the bend. He thinks: this wild,

untutored panorama proclaims my destiny, a vision of a life transformed by landscape into epic. Here is a New Aegean to kindle his pilgrim soul. In London a Midwestern kid with an Old Testament name was getting himself worked into a lather about a masculine age. He too had seen a panther, on a vase. It was palpable, you could almost touch the invisible world; its radiance thronged with the just. Had our lad returned to his New Aegean he'd have encountered

stunting implacability. Busywork would fill his days (idleness and promiscuity being the temptations that would bring the Dominion and the boys from Vimy to their knees). *C.R.M.* was discovered in a crater, swimming through pus and

single arms. He made his way to Knutsford, racing down the hill to the log house and barn he'd built with his own hands. It was cramped and dark inside. A woman and three children stood waiting. For what? The smallest ran from

him, screaming. He looked around. "How could I ever have lived here?" he asked. An impulse to dissemble came upon him, and a deep sadness. What *was* it he'd been doing here, and why? In France—in England—the hypocrisy had

been clear to see, the whole rotten system stood exposed. But here, in Kamloops, Parksville, Duncan, nothing had changed; no one knew, or if they did they acted as if they didn't. Churches and legislatures connived to contain

the damage. Had the Lord not spared the prairies and coves of His Dominion to preserve His eternal order? Here in the mystic forests, in the sober, dutiful cities, Prosthetic Man would labour selflessly once more for the success of his

betters. Came the snow and the epidemic, men found dead in their shacks, then spring again. *C.R.M.* travelled the Island looking for work. Store windows in Vancouver read: NO ENGLISH NEED APPLY. It seemed everyone who'd

stayed home was ashamed and wanted to move on. The moment for change was passing. Some sought refuge in quiescence, or killed themselves. Some raved on the streets; they were taken away. Some hearts burst, drowning

men on their pillows. Revolution, whispered some. Reds, said others. *G.A.B.*, back from France within a year with a valve that might pop on any stairwell got a government job in Ottawa. His ear froze to the trumpet of *eleisons*,

156

elisions. How precise your ribs are, ewe, your swollen belly, your neck turned as if your chin were resting on an altar's lip. Who cast you skinned you. And loved you. You alter us by that love. Aching loneliness settled over the Dominion,

man to man, woman to woman, woman to man. How do you imagine sex in such a nation? (Know yourself.) Nonie at 85 says it's what you do with your hormones that determines if there'll be peace. What you do with your

hormones determines when the Army's called up. Temperance leagues stifled free association. There was the woodshed. And the greenhouse. And the toolshed. And the pumphouse. I recall multiple ossuaries of the Black & White.

A slave in the archipelago of Mother Dao, in my father's time, recalling the days before the missions and the bosses, sang, "...*tears spring to the eyes of someone who knows the language of poetry.*" That language cannot be heard

in a slave's world—a world split in two. "*He himself is destroyed and does not know it.*" I take in my hand the talisman, the mothering ewe, cast in bronze. Whose journey to the underworld did you assist? What if the world were not

split in two? Ask the young father anchored in the narrows, half-pissed, wrenched from his night sweats by drums and flames on the spit. It's 1933. Someone has died. The cries from the village make his heart palpitate. "Fuckin'

Indians," he thinks although these are not his words. If his boys said such a thing he'd beat the hell out of them. The next moment he's sobbing. He reaches for his bottle. As for the angelic hosts at Mons, did a battalion of

the Kaiser's best with magic lanterns project cones of shimmering elohim onto the clouds above the lines? Hundreds swore they heard the heavenly choir and tore off their helmets in wonder. Man cried to man. What if it was true?

 G-PF

Somme

What does not bleed? Solvent. As Isla tells it, Joe McCulloch owned a shoe store in Strathclair, Manitoba. What age is light? A caress. He'd sit outdoors when it was fair and make smart comments when older girls passed by. What

year? She left for good in '23. No, it was Hubert Morrison they steered clear of. Eighteen, nineteen, a big boy, he told the kids one afternoon he wanted their dog—a stray collie-cross. He was just gonna grab it. So when they

spotted him they'd take off through the fields to the next farm, hearts pounding, to hide between the rows. What fear is this? Sometimes you'd find a little baby ear that was growing onto its mama. And if the heart's pouch of

moxiebustion does not ignite? She heard about the incident later, after she'd left town. It was on Hallowe'en, with an apostrophe. Her father, on his own (their mother had died in the epidemic with her baby), had never allowed

the kids out on Hallowe'en. Strathclair was too rough, he said, on Hallowe'en. This was the year of *Spring and All*, Williams frantic for an a linguistic break-through, not buttress—but breach, for a "*world detached from the necessity of*

recording it, sufficient to itself...," for a self-obliterating operation in the body of language that could be called *love*. This was no parlour trick. It was a cry for something *true*, for a *being* unhooked from the concealed and corporate layers

of hypocrisy and encumbrance, for volition and knowing exterior to language. It was life or death. And what for asymptote but language itself? She is thirteen. "How," she wonders, "will I know love?" Look to the borders, lassie.

> *It is at the edge of the*
> *petal that love waits*

Crisp, worked to defeat
laboredness—fragile
plucked, moist, half-raised
cold, precise, touching

What

The place between the petal's
edge and the

He's struggling here for *definition*, which for too long he's confused with *representation*, and with both he's stymied. He jettisons the perps. Wittgenstein, a year earlier, pacing the same crumbling shore, says

everything his language can allow then chucks away the ladder he scaled it with. He turns to face "the inexpressible", which begins at Williams' *the*. It "*shows* itself," he writes, "it is the mystical." This astonishing *shows* is the

catalyst for the journey Joe McCulloch's comrades died to prevent. Honing a receding representational edge, Williams wants to plunge beyond language into being's amnion, to become consciously *un*conscious. "The sense of the world,"

writes Wittgenstein, "must lie outside the world." To *be* then is to straddle the edges, to be perishing and giving birth to oneself each moment. It's too close for Joe McCulloch. The wind screeches off the lakes, making a mark across

Strathclair like an indelible pencil. Seems that night Hubert Morrison and some friends thought it would be a lark to plug up Joe's chimney. The apostrophe is a cold night on the prairies. Hubert and a couple of chums crawl up onto Joe's

roof and in a jiffy the job is done. Before long Joe rushes out. He's mad. Smoke pours through the door. He shouts, "Get off of my roof." He's got a rifle. Hard to say: a .22, or a .303. Hubert laughs. Maybe gives Joe the finger, it's Hallowe'en. Joe takes aim and brings his man down. That was the end of Hubert Morrison. Strays rejoice! She wasn't there then, she says, but when she was, when she passed Joe McCulloch on the street outside his shoe

store and he muttered something, what she remembers is trying to think the very best she could of him; he'd been brave over there she'd heard, so, well, you know, his wisecracks could, well, be forgiven. D.W. Griffith, "*very*

disappointed with the reality of the battlefield," shot the trench scenes for *Hearts of the World* on Salisbury Plain. Joe McCulloch likely trained there. The location came in handy a year later as an influenza cemetery. Griffith,

gazing skyward in the publicity still, christened himself Gaston de Tolignac.

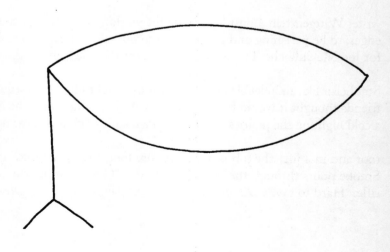

In essence, we create violence out of our memories and
not out of what is directly presented to our vision, just
as in childhood the viewer himself fills the blanks and
his own head with pictures that he manufactures a
posteriori.

Alfred Hitchcock

Passchendale

"Seven was my mother's lucky number," my mother told me on June 1st and I
wonder how many numbers and years will fall by the way if a hook doesn't lace
them to the plum swaying outside the window. Edwin, up in Alert Bay,

born there, gone away, back now, grill-cook, when he was eleven or twelve, he
told me, hooked a big halibut. But the forensic activity concentrates on the
tips of the artifact suggesting sharpness or charring may be significant. She

would call this without a smile a fine point. What she could not escape was
the full brunt, castle and keep. You are thinking cheap metaphor but there are
no metaphors in here. I am through with the pretty elegiasts and the

jockeying smirkers of America. I'd rather be a hooligan than defenestrator of
predicates where constipated dogs patrol on stilts. John Ford, teenaged in
Portland, Maine, saw the lads of the Black Watch streaming from special trains

rushed in from Windsor Station (the St. Lawrence being frozen up, the troop ships
diverted), parading through the snowbanks with pipes and sporrans swinging up
gangplanks like their fathers on the Chilcoot Pass. The artifact's end

makes little difference. He was out there most of the afternoon hauling the
thing in. It was summer, still light. An hour passed before he saw its eyes
and when they lugged it up the beach and stuck it on the scales it weighed

three hundred pounds. What was the matter with the guy I can't distinguish
from myself in the movie running down the hill in silhouette above the
ranchhouse exploding with light? Can I imagine a time before Nanton or

Waller? Is this collage hacked out of iconic pulp? Let me chew it. It is degenerate, her mother said. She'd say none of that music. I would say mine was invaded early by those she trusted, crippled by them and they steer her

still for she loves them too fiercely. All they could not speak of she must bear and she is loyal to the weight but not the plunder. You'll see what this means when the bayonet is inserted into your hip socket and rotated sharply.

They're snapshots now, twenty-five cents apiece. She is stubborn and will not forsake them. They bred her wisely. Do you remember the time she brought out the shinplaster? She'll have no histories now. "I can't care," she says.

Edwin's halibut got winched onto the lawn and his dad cut it up, throwing the heart into the long grass. Edwin that night above the restaurant took a drag, poured a glass, and swore to me it was still beating three hours later.

*One of the largest trees was felled, and its stump served
as a dance floor, while its trunk was used as a bowling
alley. The bark, stripped from the trunk, was sent to
New York City, where in 1854 it was exhibited in the
large Racket Court of the Union Club at No. 596
Broadway. The bark of another tree, christened
"Mother of the Forest", also made the long voyage via
Cape Horn for exhibition in New York. Finally, this
exhibit was shipped to England and placed on view in
London. Since no building in that city could
accommodate its full height of 116 feet, the exhibit was
dismantled for reassembly in the Crystal Palace at
Sydenham, where it remained until December of 1866,
when the palace was consumed by fire.*

Stephen A. Spongberg

Bourlon Woods

Mink and hammer

oak and cap

staple and coyote

rowan or shovel

hare or adverb

iron-lung and yarrow

Red Cap and red cap

cake and louse

straight-waistcoat and tansy

fossil or ventricle

C.R.M. said

he recalled

one thing.

What he remembered,

he said, was

watching his comrades

falling back

into the trenches,

shot down

by their own officers.

163

Smoke

2:00-5:00 PM

Disney says sadly, that Mickey now has to behave.
He never did. In the old days (which some of us still
remember) Mickey was as metaphysical as that
felicitous cat he finally chased out of films. Not so
now. His logic is literal. He is matter-of-fact.... Mickey
now is not poetry, but verse.... Meanwhile Disney has
other favourites. One is Donald Duck. He thinks he
will grow on us, and he is happy to have someone who
can be irresponsible, rude, ribald and all that Mickey
was before he became Uncle Sam's best "G" man.

Inchy

Let us ally ourselves with stones.
The lawn won long ago.

The magnificence of the herd
addressing the torn
loveliness of its limbs on the snow
gives way to shale.

What of the copper beech, radiant at dawn?
The snowberry? A bronze ewe? The glad-hearted earwig?

No thing can be divided from any other thing.
Love is meant to kill you.

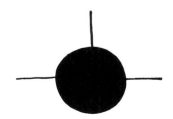

Cloven

As if by sheer effort a bay in a headland appears and the ship that enters it is
your neck which more people than you can know would have if they thought no
one was watching and as I say these words an orange and green pennant is

being hooked to a halyard and run up the mast and the breeze is stiff I can
make out intermittently the letters on it rippling: N-O   O-N-E   I-S
W-A-T-C-H-I-N-G and for the sake of propriety you take a hankie from your

sleeve and begin to dab at the open half of yourself which is professionally
drained and freshly cauterized. Some fissures weep. You roll toilet paper into
a carnation, tidy up the rough edges and feel a shape in your pocket:

the styptic pencil. May I report that his signet ring throbs? That the
monogrammed shaving kit unzips to reveal a clandestine desert city,
laid out, you realize, with its lids and boxes, its boulevards of soap-scented

leather, the gleaming, vented *faux-ivoire* barrel of its toothbrush tube, as if
it were an exemplary target, *un bijou?* The ewe's ears flutter.
Her people know this song. She lifts her head. This god too—a codpiece

in the burning air; his names sparks she dodges, his throne her incinerator,
her lamb his ossuary. Dawn bleats. You test your memory on a plate in the
fridge from the night before. The smoke rising from the human bonfires

is black and oily. Some *"clawed their mouths ceaselessly." "Another sucked
a rubber tube fastened to the gas-jet."* A mother on the northern border, in
the town with the ice rink and Zamboni, has set herself on fire.

A crow jeers at a frozen puddle.

We step out into glory.

Heir is bot twynklyng of ane e

How many ways can one be torn in two? A girl extends her hand. In the distance the black hill seems ideal, rising and falling like the belly of an upturned deer in the scented evening. There is something that seems to have become

seamless and it troubles the vulnerable waters of the lake upon which my craft discharges the stain of itself. I am trying to put it into words but they elude us here where the grass looks as if something or someone has slept the

night despite the rain which was not all that persuasive if you recall. The first rain of summer is mnemonia, a sound-effect, where glistening shafts were. The table, its matchstick and mouse, the Malcolmy tolling of the glass lid in the

dishwasher, the great swaying trees beyond us at the beach, their tops dying into sticks. What do you expect sowbugs to eat? Why do we say we do not understand? What is there to not understand. What is not us? Fire is wax is

nectar is bee is shit is earth is wheat is bread, and every cell is holy. I want to hide when the world greens. It is as if the children in the playground far below are once more forming letters with their bodies. And this cockpit of swarming

apparitions? Colin (*C.R.N.*), George (*G.A.B.*), Dick, Enid, Marjorie, Nora, Herbert, Molly, Harriet, Marie, in your sun hats, Sam Browns and neckerchiefs, it's time. Your photographs in the albums with Indian Chiefs burned into the deerskin

are disintegrating. I will keep your occasions and your names, and your loves alive, such as I know them. The children are circling the alley pots. Let us hold hands one more time, in our circle. Take a deep breath. Now, let go

August 15, 1999, Maple Bay, B.C.

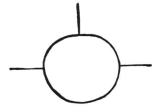

Seed Limit (A Consolation)

For Clare, nouned in cowslips, it's an emergency.
Each verb
a ledge.

The mountain liquifies and shrieks into the valley
and he is the man placing stones in its way to contain it.
That mountain is his beloved and those stones his reason.
Amichai? I see him bending over the desert
searching for a young poet
who fought in the battle of Huleikat.

> I have lost my outrider.
> Nothing anchors me.

Spring and All is an emergency.
The vowel is transparent; the doctor
has put his finger through it.
He utters a hedge. Stop!
And Clare, sowing, naming as the meadows vanish.
Klein, roaming the alphabets
in torment impenetrable.
Dies Irae.

A spring clip designed like a man? The *dotterel*, Clare might say
assigning *throstles* to *chicker*.
How did the English get Canute so wrong?
What story is not a weapon?

> I have lost my outrider.
> My gyro's agley.

Waddell's *Psalms: Frae Hebrew intil Scottis* is an emergency.
In the auld buik
the faithful are torn in three.

The head's in Jerusalem
the bunion's in Oxford
the willy's in Aberdeen.

Waddell's scheme: to improvise a fantastic gynandromorphic clone,
a melodious freak, a habitable whole
with the crown of King David, Burns' loins
and a fondness for figs and kippers. The tongue
shapes the world.
Do ye not ken Hermon
on that hilum?

> *Thar's the saft seep o' the cluds an' the dour chirt o' the
> cranreuch; the lown holms, the green knowes, an' the blythe
> braes o' Bethle'm; the cauld dyke-side, the snell showir, an'
> the snaw-white tap o' Lebanon; thar's the wimplin' burn, the
> rowin spate, an' the gran' walth o' watirs; thar's the lanely,
> drowthy, dreich wustlan; thar's the lowan heugh, the bleezan
> cairn, an' the craig that lowps an' dinnles; thar's the glint o'
> mony starn, the bright light o' the lift, an' the dule o' the
> dead-mirk dail, thegither; thar's the sang of the cheerie herd,
> the sigh o' the weary wight, the maen o' the heartbroken man,
> an' the eerie sugh o' the seer; the dirl o' the pipe, the chirm
> o' the bird, the tout o' the swesch, an' the scraigh o' thunner;
> the mither's lilt for her wean, an' heigh hozannas at the yetts
> o' hevin: what the ee can see, what the lug can carrie; the chant
> o' the sant, an' the dule gant o' the godlowse; the blythe-bid o'
> the Lord himsel, an' the angrie ban o' his servan—foregather'd
> a intil this ae Buik—ane gran' melee.*

Under the ice, a blizzard of swirling mud
thoraxes and claws, pieces of night.
I look up into an eagle's face.
At my feet: pine needles, hair balls.

A single explosion, 10 billion years ago!
Within a few millionths of a second
something was "filled with a fiery sea
of particles that scientists
refer to...as a quark-gluon plasma." (NYT)

What was there to be filled, mother?

Pollard a tree.
Emergency.
It panicks, flowers, fruits, shoots seeds,
Clare, Klein, Williams, Amichai
Folks are but frute-stoks...
Waddell: the bush he burns.

You are a young man of Bremen. In North Africa you took from
strangers what you would not wish to give yourself. You march out of the
desert exhausted and humiliated under armed guard. You board a
freighter for the New World and lie in a nausea. You board a train in the
night and it rattles and whines through the snow for days while you nod
off, dreaming of Red Indians. You enter the Lethbridge compound at
dawn. The sky is red. You are assigned a bunk. You are a spoil of His
Majesty. You devour three of the 39,000 meals prepared each day. Here,
after fourteen months, you find you cannot take your eyes off a
Nordstrand farm boy with a chest. During the summer you rake hay in a
farmer's field stripped to the waist. He glistens. While dipping a mug of
water into a pail one afternoon your lips brush the boy's back as he rises
with his own scoop. Now you cannot live without seeing him. How shy
and happy you are becoming! You notice yourself reflected in windows.
Your mother's letters make you impatient. You've forgotten you are a son.
One night in the cinema you drop your head onto his shoulder, laughing.
He does not move away. Now you cannot stop talking, you're giddy. The
blizzard shrieks all night Huge flakes drive past the floodlights, piling up
in jewelled hills. How gentle he is. *Dies Irae.* That night the S.S. visit you

and before you are fully awake they take you into the toilet and snap your
neck. You are thrown out into the snowbank where the Canadians will
identify you in a few days, after the Chinook, after the emergency.

Puddles of sky, puddles of beaks.
Emergencies riddle the sod.
Here is one of the great exchanges:
worms, drowning in their chambers,
rise simultaneously to become
in milli-seconds
birds.

When they gathered on that final evening
just down the road from here
the animals knew. Even the dog-like one.
Famine, inquisition, plague, they foresaw;
confusion, extortion, disjunction,
the treacheries of language.
In short, they foresaw their replacements.
Let's forget our differences, they said,
let's reminisce about the early days
and the grandeur of our intentions.
Some fell to embracing.
Some scuffled.
Let us bid each other a warm farewell.
Then words evaporated from them.

What is more beautiful than your head thrown back and a song pouring out
of your mouth? Every day God speaks to millions. What is wrong with you?
You could become an oriole.

How does one prepare for the great exchange?
On a morning like this you need skates.

What of the storm of ash?
Something the size of the pond
has been sleeping in the rushes.
Look up.
You'll see what's hunting you.

        I have lost my outrider.
        If you should see a black dog
        if you should see a beach where
        a black dog ran...
        she was the wind's flag.
        She was my heart's heart.
        Dies Irae.

Gaze up through the fiery plasma. Refracted through ice
a man
is leaning over
placing stones in his pockets.

The oscillation of the tongue
is the waveshape of the world,
its orison.

        WAVE
        WARE
        WORE
        WORM
        WARM
        WART
        WORT
        WORD

21 August 2001

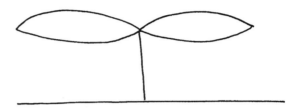

Returning Late
for Peter Quartermain

*...grasping one's own mind in its action. In this way, the
sphere of consciousness gained a new territory.*
      J.G. Fichte, *Foundations of Natural Right* (1796)

Finches, inches away
in the wisteria, their
mess, you said
they stay awake
all night

or a little spotted owl
a frozen priest
a cedar bowl
unburrowed

an avenue lined with plane trees
that resemble giant squid
plunging into the earth

manifestations

one with black wings
cruises nurseries
sober her triage

one can't be bothered
lets the cat go
wings can be weapons

what a bushy tail!

Magnolia, am I Anglo?
Sink, or skin?

...grasping one's own mind
in its action...

An attack on a skirmish?

In this way, the sphere of consciousness
gained a new territory

Pray, predator.

Fichte's ambushing orb, an egg
called liberty in a mental nest,
declares itself with startling
(or starling) candour, its analogue
being Melville's score-settling
"Paul Jones of nations."

When the shell is broken
there is no going back.
Honour and a genius for
humiliation and savagery
pour forth
as they always do.
The trusting are led away in triumph
in manacles.

I, apparently, is the nation's excuse,
its "improving" angel.

A hand, a creel
a lamb, an eel
viburnum
viaticum

their wings
at night
I hear them
swing
in there

little birds
where will you sleep?

My father's wings, and his before him
vast inner
fluttering

who he
who he
who he

his heat,
mine now.

A viaticum for
you, Dad.

24 November 2000 – 24 March 2002

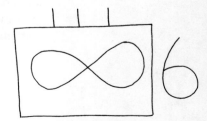

Entrance
for Judith Mastai

This hunger for consolation. Don't be frightened.
I am frightened.
It's a crow with its fierce beak
tearing apart a coleslaw cup.
Hopping onto a pot of Bear's Claw
a Dark-eyed Junco snatches a seed.
Dark-eyed, for the flame burning there.

In a grove,
on the rim of the desert's white mouth,
in the civil dust of catkins
that flame.
It burns in a child like a lantern in a mind.
The mind is your father's dark bedroom seventy years ago
when he was a boy.
The flame burning in you.

Listen, the deaf man's last quartets.
Our house is stacked with envelopes and boxes;
we are afraid to let them go.
Sleep is a consolation, a kindness,
a happy cannibalism.
Consciousness is appetite,
not kind-hearted.
How many lanterns will this poem extinguish?

How do I approach the border? Who speaks with me?

I hurry down to the wood, heavy with grief.
It's dark. The branches stream with water.
I greet myself as a child, we pass one another
in the startling air.
Alders bloom. My parents arrive. A duck

stands in the sky on the path at the forest door.
In a young cottonwood
an immature iggle swings, or so Rothenberg
might say. Leaves hankie canes.
A dog's ghost
chases a squirrel in the oaks.
Mergansers are hunted
by a crow.
The old guy in the Mother Tree
unwraps his length of cord.
The beaver lifts a stick.
My father approaches
with my infant daughter in his arms.
Under the trees the cohorts
shape the air with their voices.
Such bargaining!
Judith, you'd ask, *What's this all about?*
You'd say, *We can do better than this.*

An owl regains its perch as if a film were reversed.
Imagine that dark bedroom in every detail:
wallpaper, the lamp shades with belaying pin and wheels,
the secret drawer.

In pods seeds rattle, greedy for water.
The sun is greedy for their roots,
rain for their thirst,
butterfly for the green flame,
eye for the petal, bee for the juice,
tick for its swaying tower,
wind to rattle it.

Behind me the dark-eyed land
is burning. How can I say I'm only playing
at being here?

20 April / 21 August 2001, Vancouver, B.C.

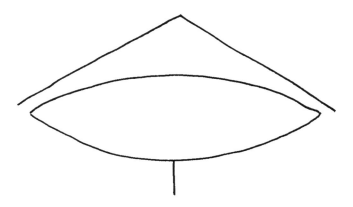

The Missions

*"'This is a song I stole from my sister,' an Indian explained to me,
as he told how he had helped collect and translate songs to be
used in a musical production based on Indian life—a production
managed by a capable teacher in the Indian day school and
performed for White audiences. 'It's her song about feeling lonely
when her parents died.' Another was a neighbour's song of
weeping for the dead; another, his own brother's song about how
sad he had felt when he was in the army, away from his songs."*

i

A flag.　Salute.

ii

I caught this morning morning's mannequins of culture, the puritans,
pedants and poetry wonks, the dewy laureates, finger-waggers,
human mimosas, monks of the metronome, Zambonis of the soul,
surfacing the dead air with platitudes, enforcing enthusiasm
and insipid self-promotion.　Quarantine me, *s.v.p.*　À bas
High-Anglican metaphysical ipecac, aggressive social ambition and false
modesty posing as altruism (that opportunistic strain of trench fever
in which missionaries and poets portray the lice).

These fraying ropes and god-eaters, they're my kin?

iii

An organ dropped into a tub of cold water
blooms.　All things bloom.

On the beach at Penelakut on the Trincomali side
of Kuper Island, I'm told, two cedar logs lay in the rain for years.

In Sussita two perfect rows of Tuscan columns lie heavily on their own
shadows on the evangelical tiles and shell casings.
Down the rockslide at Kursi ordinary swine minding their own beeswax
became another screw to the thumbs of the non-believers.
A cheap shot? They were morphed into
howling pig lunatics. To hide their shame they flung themselves
into the wintry Galilee.

One blistering summer afternoon on the beach one of the logs
cracked open. Out came a man. Not long after
from the place between the logs a woman appeared.
Wiping the sand off she must have wondered, *Who are you?*

High in the saddle at Sussita the ribbed, coiled casings
of centipedes, *nadal*, in Hebrew, little black buttons on the hillside,
and on the reverse of the sign warning of landmines
a hand-written question: *Are you a vandal?*
Please replace the soil on the cathedral floor.

iv

The TV reporter cornered the chief from Squamish.
"What do you people want?" she asked. "If all this land
is *yours*, what can *we* expect?"

"A fair settlement," he said.

"Look at it this way," he said, "Title to this land
was never ceded by us to anyone." And he gestured
to the lopped trunks in Stanley Park and the fibreglass totem poles,

the reflections of international gasoline barges in Coal Harbour.
"This," he said, "is our Jerusalem."

v

My neighbour asks over a flute of local Pinot Gris on a late summer
evening, "How else would you have it? Look, we too are victims;
here are our scars." Mably, in his *Recherches historiques et politiques sur les
Etats-Unis de l'Amerique septentrionale* (1788): "...the liberty which every
European believes himself to enjoy is nothing but the possibility of
breaking his chain in order to give himself up to a new master."

Tonight we'll revisit each other's wounds again. The neighbour advises,
"Choose peace, my friend; justice is just too messy."

vi

> So that on what we
> realized might be
> the last time we'd
>
> scrape ice off our windshield
> in the twentieth century
> it was sunny and bright
>
> and because she was to
> dance her new solo
> to the oboe theme
>
> in *The Mission*
> for the first time
> in competition

that afternoon
in Burnaby
and was anxious

yet composed and
looking forward to it,
having practiced that

morning on the carpet
in the den where
the dog sleeps

watching our bed
for signs of life,
I dropped my daughter

off at school
under the trees
and before she joined

the girls
pushing through
the chain-link gate

my lips said,
"God bless you,"
and she said,

"That's what Gran
said last night."
I can't speak

for my mother
but I've never
said that before.

vii

"The value of a uniform in the Services need not be dwelt upon.
There would be no true cohesion without a uniform. Further,
if modern Dictators find that a coloured shirt assists in
implanting political doctrines and even racial and theological
ideas, it should be obvious that the adoption of a bright and
attractive uniform would assist in implanting all that we desire
in the children under our care."

viii

My body's in the way now. It seemed so happy in the Navy
following orders, serving its Lord: spoken for, fussed over,
indulged, tested, timed, made sleek, flexible, hairless, hard. Each day
it led me forth, loved for itself alone, its shrug, its length, its constancy,
its crush on the R.S.M., its octennial indenture.
That was my youth. I was a bride.

ix

4 crows
&
a rat
on its back
 its toes
 in the air

184

its belly
a red hole
they're yarding
organs
out of

a long sandy
bloom
pulled out
in the sun
at the high tide
mark.

x

How can they have remained passive as little children, stripped of songs,
washed up on their beaches? My parents, and theirs,
and their sisters and brothers, and theirs?
How do I, and mine, behave? I lie until I don't know I am lying anymore.
Such conviction makes for a respectable, even beloved nation.

xi

Do you remember Carmen McRae, with Dave Brubeck and Paul Desmond,
singing "Strange Meadowlark"? I have found its valley and this barn is its ear.

In a letter Ronald Duncan sent to the old evangelist in St. Elizabeth's
the day I was born, he recounts visits to Cocteau, Brancusi and Bérard.
That same morning Dorothy wrote from Rapallo, thrilled
that a Red Cross sister had shown up with a tin of peanut butter.
British military "poleece" had grilled her the day before in Genova,
she complained. "The Brits are an unpleasant lot, except ones friends!"

Driving across the rainy city, I remember the brown eyes
on my mother's chest watching me watching her in her bath.

Will there be a memorial for 'Ou=bee', the little Beothuk girl
who survived an intertribal raid in the Bay of Exploits in 1791
and who was rescued by the Stones, a family of British
exhibitionists who took her across the sea where she perished
four years later but not before telling Lt. George Christopher Pulling
as many words she could think of, 110 views of the world without Mt. Moriah?

This is the valley, and the barn. The old man, who much preferred
his flocks and the summer range, hid from his daughters here.
Pixillating sun. Percheron hills. The grass was waist-high, a harvester
told me. "It was like the sea," she said, "when the wind blows."
She'd fetch her kids up here for the bitterroot in May.
That father in the stalls on a February afternoon with snow flying, a
mickey, and night falling fast. "Catched," he thinks, "I am the animal now."

A human spine towers over the hill, a cloud
lit by a falling sun.

28 May 2002

ewe's love
a glove

ram's face
a carapace

lamb's fit
a spit

ewe's bleat
a cleat

ram's hill
smoking still

lamb's glee
a .303

lamb's glans
a man's

ewe

I found her one afternoon
in the Persian

Arts, a little
bronze casting,

wary, her head
held forward

slight, a psalm
sung by a herdsman's

hands, gentle,
lamb weary

her brow a clock
of $CuSO_4$.

At the age of 29, the mother
of a son and the young wife

of the British ambassador
to Constantinople,

Lady Mary Wortley Montagu,
sent, by hand, a "little box"

to her dear friend Lady _____
(who'd asked for a Greek slave).

It was, she wrote, a "Turkish love-letter"
seventeen verses long,

each "verse" embodied by a tiny
object. First, the beloved

withdraws a pearl. It salutes her;
"*Fairest of the young,*" it declares.

Reaching in again she, or he might
pull out a little brown peg.

"*You are as slender as this clove!*"
croons the ardent peg. "*You are*

an unblown rose! I have long loved you,
and you have not known it!"

Lady Mary, who'd accompanied
women in the streets

gathering and inoculating
their infants against

the small-pox with pus
and nut-shells, and slitting tools

like Abraham's—"engrafting"
she called it—was tickled pink

by this love tongue of things.
"There is no colour," she exclaimed,

"no flower, no weed, no fruit, herb,
pebble, or feather, that has not

a verse belonging to it; and you may
quarrel, reproach, or send letters of

passion, friendship, or civility,
or even of news without ever

inking your fingers." In mine,
a Bronze Age ewe,

a pouring of copper, tin,
silica & altar fire.

*"You are an unopened rose!
A skunk cabbage!"* she bleats.

*"You with your severed head,
your dead god,*

*your past and future,
your thorns and trinkets*

*and wheels of crows,
careening*

*through winter skies,
I am your bride.*

*In the furnace of your
soaring wound I was*

*engrafted. I'll be with you
when your empire*

returns as someone's lint.
Forget yourself. The wild hyacinth's

in bloom, smoke billows from
altars all along the sea,

my milk's sweet, my god lives,
come, follow me."

Ewe, we'll dance
strategically; you

indivisible, imperishable,
radiant beyond the stench, and me,

son, heir and salient
of the incubating trench.

12 March 2002

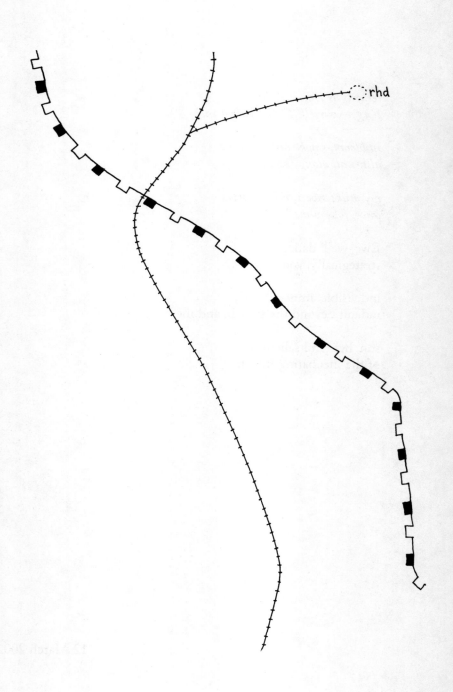
rhd

NOTES

Ground Water

Ground Water was first performed at the Vancouver Art Gallery by Martin Gotfrit and Colin Browne in April 1988, thanks to an invitation from Judith Mastai. It was subsequently performed in Montréal, Toronto, Ottawa, Victoria and, in July 1989, at the Hornby Festival on Hornby Island, B.C. Many thanks to Tom Durrie. Martin Gotfrit wrote and performed all the music. He is in every way a thoughtful and generous collaborator. I owe him a huge debt of thanks.

Page 11. *"The trees went forth on a time to anoint a king over them..."*: Judges 9: 8–15. The aristocrats choose a strong man.

Page 11. *"locus ille locorum"*: Alan de Lille, *Anticlaudianus*, the 'place of places.' Cited in E.R. Curtius, *European Literature and the Latin Middle Ages*, trans. Willard R. Trask (Princeton: Bollingen/Princeton University Press, 1953), 198. Alan de Lille thus describes the natural grove which represents the highest form of pastoral beauty; evidence, perhaps, of Paradise.

Page 11. *"...golden dishes...golden cups..."*: The Koran, 43: 65

Page 11. *"Rivers at their feet"*: The Koran, 16: 28.

Page 11. *"Dicite, quandoquidem in molli consedimus herbe"*: Virgil, *Eclogues*, III, line 55. 'Begin your song, now that we're well seated on soft grass.'

Page 11. *"...y aparacen las sendas / impenetrables"*: Federico García Lorca, "La Luna Asoma": '...and the impenetrable paths appear.' J.L. Gili, ed. & trans., *Lorca* (Harmondsworth: Penguin Books, 1960), 26.

Page 12. *"locus amoenus"*: A 'lovely place', a pleasance; an uncultivated pastoral paradise in Roman poetry, i.e., a rhetorical device.

Page 12. *"Amnis ibat inter herbas valle fusus frigida..."*: Tiberianus, translated in Curtius, (196), as "Through the fields there went a river; down the airy glen it wound...." Airy glen strikes the right note.

Page 12. *"For I would only ask thereof / That thy worm should be my worm, Love"*: Thomas Hardy, "1967". His is also the Second Edition, in this case the Thin Paper Edition of *Collected Poems of Thomas Hardy*, Vol. 1 of *The Poetical Works of Thomas Hardy* (London: Macmillan and Co., 1928), 204.

Page 12. *"Bomb craters visible on the streets, simply fabulous..."*: Lieutenant Colonel Wolfram von Richthofen, to his diary, after bombing

Guernica, April 26th, 1937. Cited in Peter Wyden, *The Passionate War* (New York: Simon and Schuster, 1983), 359.

Page 13. *"Don't sit under the apple tree with anyone else but me..."*: The first line from a song made famous by the Andrews Sisters during the Second World War.

Page 14. *"Nunc frondent silvae, nunc formosissimus annus"*: Virgil, *Eclogues*, III, line 57: 'Now is the forest coming into leaf, now is the year at its most fair.'

Page 14. *"I thought it the fairest land I had ever set eyes on... strawberries"*: Hugh Mackenzie, [Reminiscences] (Victoria: British Columbia Provincial Archives, n.d.). Mackenzie recalls the words of William Thompson, the first European settler to farm the valley that descends to Hagen Creek on the Saanich Peninsula (1855).

Page 14. *"Sint in eo diversae arbores et fructus in eis dependentes..."*: From the stage directions of an Anglo-French mystery play about Adam: "There are [in paradise] many different trees, and fruit dangling in them...." Curtius, 200.

Page 14. *"...providing employment...leisure...what it is you want...,"* etc.: These and the following excerpts within quotation marks, with the exception of the wife's lines, are from C.H. Douglas, *The Use of Money* (London: Stanley Nott Ltd., 1934). The words selected are those written or underlined by a man known locally as 'the Major' who built his utopian house and garden in Saanichton during the 1920s. He became a follower of the economic theories of Major Douglas and an unsuccessful Social Credit candidate for the provincial legislature in the 1940s.

Page 14. *"Amoenitatis locus"*: St. Boniface called Paradise 'the loveliest of places.' Curtius, 200.

Page 14. *"...worried by the dogs..."*: Arnold Lunn, *Spanish Rehearsal*, 97. Quoted in the Duchess of Atholl, *Searchlight on Spain*, 3rd ed. (Harmondsworth: Penguin Books, 1938), 108.

Page 15. *"La gloria di colui che tutto move / per l'universo penetra..."*: Dante, *Paradiso*, Canto 1, lines 1–2: "The glory of the One who sets everything in motion penetrates the universe...."

Page 15. *"...te, dulcis coniunx, te solo in litore..."*: Virgil, *Georgics* IV, line 465. Orpheus: "...you, sweet wife, you alone on the desolate shore...."

Page 15. *"Wherever you looked we saw nothing but targets and more targets."*: Oberleutnant Harro Harder, Nazi Condor Legion pilot in Spain, July 25, 1937. Wyden, 384.

Page 16.   *"CREATING...assuming for the moment that we have the power to do,"* etc.: The words within quotation marks are from C.H. Douglas, *The Use of Money*, and are those underlined or glossed by 'the Major', the book's owner.

Page 16.   *"Nature and education..."*: A phrase taken from a description of Lord Plymouth, chairman of the Non-Intervention Committee, by Ivan Maisky, Soviet Ambassador to London in 1936. See Paul Preston, *The Spanish Civil War, 1936–39* (London: Weidenfeld and Nicholson, 1986), 83.

Page 16.   *"I was no bachelor and I knew if I were to succeed...mind"*: Hugh Mackenzie, in his [Reminiscences], recalls William Thompson describing his marriage in 1856.

Page 17.   *"il miglior fabbro"*: "The better craftsman" or, in the older sense of the word, "maker," or poet. With this inscription, first bestowed by Dante upon the Provençal troubadour Arnaut Daniel, T.S. Eliot dedicated the first appearance of *The Waste Land* in 1922 to his friend Ezra Pound (1885–1972). By 1922 Pound was actively promoting Major C.H. Douglas and his Social Credit economic theories. That same year his translation of Remy de Gourmont's *The Natural Philosophy of Love* appeared. de Gourmont seems to have encouraged Pound in his belief that men's brains, as instruments of generation, were creatively stimulated by the production of sperm, via the spinal cord, into the skull.

Page 19.   *"We are not afraid of ruins; we are going to inherit the earth"*: Buenaventura Durriti, Anarchist militia leader killed on the Madrid front in November, 1936. Preston, 4.

Page 19.   *"Sic euntem per virecta pulchra odora et musica / Ales amnis aura lucus flos et umbra iuverat"*: Tiberianus, cited in Curtius, 196: 'To a wanderer in the beautiful thicket filled with song and scent, / Bird and river, breeze and woodland, flower and shade brought ravishment.'

Page 19.   *"The lemon trees...of Malaga"*: The reference is to Lorca.

Page 19.   *"It is a sort of contest to see who can massacre more..."*: An Italian diplomat to Mussolini in response to the savage reprisals carried out in Malaga by both sides, during the spring of 1937. Wyden, 259.

Page 26.   *"In war one becomes a jackal"*: Buenaventura Durutti, cited in Wyden, 23.

Page 26.   *"Vedi lo sol che 'n fronte ti riluce / vedi l'erbette, i fiori e li arbuscelli / che qui la terra sol da sé produce"*: Dante, *Purgatorio*, XXVII, lines 133–135: 'Look at the sun that shines upon your brow; look at the grasses, flowers, and the shrubs born here, spontaneously, of the earth....' Trans. Allen Mandelbaum, *Purgatorio: A Verse Translation* (Toronto: Bantam Books, 1984), 108–109.

Page 26. *"...la divina foresta spessa e viva..."*: Dante, *Purgatorio*, XXVIII, line 2: "...that forest—dense, alive with green, divine...." Mandelbaum, 254–5. Mandelbaum, 258–9.

Page 27. *"Intrate; ma facciovi accorti / che di fuor torna chi 'n dietro si guata."*: Dante, *Purgatorio*, IX, lines 131–132: 'Enter; but I warn you—he / who would look back, returns—again—outside" (on entering the gate of Purgatory). Mandelbaum, 108–9.

Page 28. *"...hermosa viril / que en montes de carbón, anuncios y ferrocarriles, / soñabas ser un río y dormir como un río..."*: Lorca, "Oda a Walt Whitman", Gili, 83: "...virile beauty, who in mountains of coal, posters, and railways, dreamed of being a river and sleeping like a river...."

Page 28. *"Vengo a buscar lo que busco, / mi alegría y mi persona."*: Lorca, "Romance de la Pena Negra", Gili, 47.

Page 28. *"...eese de meen krupsasa loho...panta"*: Hesiod, *Theogony*, 162–3: spoken of Kronos.

Page 29. *"...hombre solo en el mar..."*: Lorca, "Oda a Walt Whitman", Gili, 84: "...lone man in the sea...."

Page 29. *"Agonía, agonía, sueño, fermento y sueño. Este es el mundo, amigo, agonía, agonía"*: Lorca, "Oda a Walt Whitman", Gili, 85: "Agony, agony, dream, ferment and dream. Such is the world, my friend, agony, agony."

Page 30. *"...te, dulcis coniunx, te solo in litore, / te veniente die, te decendente..."*: Virgil, *Georgics*, IV, lines 465–6. Orpheus, to Eurydice.

Blondin!

Page 34. Blondin's dream is taken from Shane Peacock, *The Great Farini: The High-Wire Life of William Hunt* (Toronto: Penguin Books, 1995), 40.

Page 36. *"Lord of the Hempen Realm!"*: This title was bestowed by *The New York Times*, Feb. 23, 1897. Peacock, 38.

Little Pinkie

Page 39. *"...e fuor di quella / è defettivo ciò ch'è lì perfetto"*: Dante, *Paradiso*, Canto XXXIII, lines 104–5: "...what appears to be perfect outside [that light], is defective."

Lunatick Bawling

Page 49.   *"To make of a long siege a short narration"*: From Richard Hakluyt, *The Principall Navigations, Voyages, Traffiques & Discoveries of the English Nation Made by Sea or Overland to the Remote & Farthest Distant Quarters of the Earth at any time within the compasse of these 1600 Yeares*, Volume II. First published in 1598. (London: J.M. Dent & Company/Everyman's Library edition, 1907), 430.

Page 49.   *"...dear old flag"*: This and the later references in italics are from Carolyn S. Bailey, "The Old Flag", in William H. Elson and William S. Gray, *The Elson Basic Readers: Book One* (Toronto: W.J. Gage & Co., Limited/Thomas Nelson & Sons, Limited, 1946).

Page 52.   At the end of Volume II, Hakluyt offers the following account. Henry's death occurred in 1413.

> [King Henrie the fourth] was taken with his last sicknesse, while he was making his prayers at Saint Edwards shrine, there as it were, to take his leave, and so to proceede foorth on his journey. He was so suddenly and grievously taken, that such as were about him feared least he would have died presently : wherefore to relieve him, if it were possible, they bare him into a chamber, that was next at hand, belonging to the Abbot of Westminster, where they layd him on a pallet before the fire, and used all remedies to revive him. At length he recovered his speech, and perceiving himselfe in a strange place which he knew not, he willed to knowe if the chamber had any particular name, whereunto answere was made, that it was called Jerusalem. Then sayde the king, Laudes be given to the father of heaven: for now I knowe that I shall die here in this chamber, according to the prophesie of mee declared, that I should depart this life in Jerusalem (461).

Five Translations

Page 53.   These translation are the result of a wonderful collaboration with composer and pipa player extraordinaire Qiu Xia He. We worked on them together and performed them, along with other songs and compositions, in a show entitled "An Evening of Chinese Music and Poetry" in Wayne Ngan's garden on Hornby Island on August 3 & 4, 1991. On the second night a storm blew up and everything had to be moved inside. Thank you to Qiu Xia, Tom Durrie and the Hornby Festival.

Altar

Page 61.   This text was published in an earlier form in *The Capilano Review*, November 1996. Thank you to Bob Sherrin, who was editor at the time. It forms the basis for a narration for a film entitled *Altar* which is currently in production. The film focuses on a photograph of the ship's company of HMCS *Mayflower* on a jetty in the dockyard in Halifax, Nova Scotia, on a morning in 1941 or 1942. A Flower Class corvette, the *Mayflower* was very likely sailing that evening with its convoy, heading out across the North Atlantic to Iceland or Britain, or Murmansk. My father was the ship's captain at the time. He was twenty-four years old.

Page 66.   *"...discipline is to an army what honour is to a woman..."*: Dave Lamb, *Mutinies: 1917–1920* (Oxford & London: Solidarity, n.d.), 23.

Page 69.   *"The Soldier's Dilemma"*: Burrell M. Singer & Lieut.-Colonel R.J.S. Langford, *Handbook of Canadian Military Law* (Toronto: The Copp Clark Company Limited, 1941), 35.

Page 71.   *"The basin and its stand of bronze..."*: Exodus 38: 8. The Revised English Bible with the Apocrypha (Oxford & Cambridge: Oxford University Press and Cambridge University Press, 1989).

Page 71.   *"...turban(s) of fine linen..."*: Exodus 39: 27–29.

Page 73.   *"Every person subject to military law..."*: Singer & Langford, 232–233.

Page 73.   *"The world is a corpse eater..."*: The Gospel of Philip: II, 3. James M. Robinson (ed.), *The Nag Hammadi Library* (San Francisco: Harper & Row, Publishers, 1977), 144.

Page 77.   *"When the young voyager plots his course..."*: R.S. Sherman & E.W. Reid, *The Canadian Industrial Reader* (Toronto: J.M Dent and Sons, Ltd., 1929), 320.

Page 77.   *"You are the knights errant..."*: "Princess Elizabeth Responds to the Toast by the Governor-General of Canada" in *The Royal Tour: Canada 1951* (Toronto: The Ryerson Press, 1952), n.p.

Page 79.   *"Every person is subject to military law..."*: Singer & Langford, 233.

Page 80.   *"An Indian pupil is hard to teach..."*: Sherman & Reid, 312.

Page 82.   *"There are three main classes of immigrant..."*: Sherman & Reid, 289–290.

Page 83.   *"...to make the castle of Liebenstein fast and impregnable..."*: Edward Burnett Tylor, *The Origins of Culture* (Gloucester, Mass.: Peter Smith, 1970), 104–105.

Page 84.   *"Every person who is subject to military law..."*: Singer & Langford, 235–236.

Page 86.   *"When a chief is greatly dissatisfied..."*: Sherman & Reid, 313.

Page 86.   *"Under the dappling summer leaves in Katyn forest..."*: See Mikhail Heller & Aleksandr M. Nekrich, *Utopia in Power: The History of the Soviet Union from 1917 to the Present* (New York: Touchstone / Simon & Schuster, 1992), 405.

Page 90.   *"The world came about through a mistake..."*: The Gospel of Philip: II, 3, 145.

Page 93.   *"Put an X opposite the most correct statement..."*: Sherman & Reid, 346.

Page 93.   *"There were three buildings specifically for sacrifice in Jerusalem..."*: The Gospel of Philip: II, 3, 142.

Page 96.   *"We have come upon beautiful lakes full of fish..."*: "Across the Mountains to Williams Lake," *Kamloops Wawa* (Kamloops, B.C., St. Louis Mission, September 1895), n.p. The Aboriginal people were regularly encouraged to pray for more priests. In a note on the first page of the February, 1895, edition of *Kamloops Wawa*, a gathering at Douglas Lake is described: "150 Indians live in the neighborhood, and most of them assembled for the eighth of December, on which feast the B. Sacrament was exposed all day, and adorators succeeded each other for the purpose of obtaining the blessings of Heaven on the missions, and an increase of missionaries."

Page 97.   *"God is a man-eater..."*: The Gospel of Philip: II, 3, 138.

Page 99.   *"...an electric washing machine, six hot plates..."*: *The Victoria Daily Colonist*, September 1943, n.d. HMCS *Orkney* was commissioned on September 18, 1943.

Presents (for a 55er)

Page 123. The role of poet Billy Little should be acknowledged in the composition of this text. It was he who called for poems to celebrate the fifty-fifth birthday of bpNichol, and I regret I did not complete this in time to send it to him.

White Bird, Dark Sea

Page 133. Dedicated to poet and scholar Charles Watts (July 10, 1948–August 5, 1998) who deserved to outlive us all.

Page 135. The references to Kaname Izumi giving candies and gum to the kids at the Kuper Island Residential School (144) and the reef named *Gakkonomae* (252) are both taken from Catherine Lang's *O-Bon in Chimunesu: A Community Remembered* (Vancouver: Arsenal Pulp Press, 1996).

Page 139. Preposition adjective adjective noun pronoun verb noun: "For one final moment we have sun."

As If

Lens

Page 143. *"The singing in opera..."*: Stanley Cavell, "Opera and the Lease of Voice", in *A Pitch of Philosophy: Autobiographical Exercises* (Cambridge: Harvard University Press, 1994), 144.

Page 143. *Floridus*: See Sir John Mandeville's *Travels*, which first appeared, in French, about 1356. Pilgrimages to the Holy Land were wildly popular at the time. The translation below is from C.W.R.D. Moseley, ed. and trans., *The Travels of Sir John Mandeville* (Harmondsworth: Penguin Books, 1983), 74–75.

> Between the church and the city [of Bethlehem] is the Field *Floridus*; it is called 'Field of Flowers' because a young maiden was falsely accused of fornication, for which cause she was to have been burnt in that place. She was led thither and bound to the stake and faggots of thorns and other woods were laid round her. When she saw the wood begin to burn, she prayed to Our Lord that as she was not guilty of that crime He would help and save her, so that all men might know it. When she had thus prayed, she entered into the fire—and immediately it went out, and those branches that were alight became red rose-trees, and those that had not caught became white ones, full of blooms. And those were the first roses and rose-bushes that were ever seen. And thus was the maiden saved by the grace of God.

Page 143. The *four kinds of wood* referred to are cypress, cedar, palm and olive, the woods traditionally used to construct the cross on which Christ was crucified. The second chapter of Mandeville's *Travels* is dedicated to this subject. Moseley, 46–49.

Vimy

Page 146. *"As man's first motives for speaking..."*: Jean-Jacques Rousseau & Johann Gottfried Herder, "Essay on the Origin of Languages." Jean-

Jacques Rousseau and Johann Gottfried Herder, *On the Origin of Languages* (Chicago: University of Chicago Press, 1966), 12.

Cambrai

Page 148. *"Upon meeting others, a savage man..."*: Jean-Jacques Rousseau & Johann Gottfried Herder, "Essay on the Origin of Languages." Jean-Jacques Rousseau and Johann Gottfried Herder, *On the Origin of Languages* (Chicago: University of Chicago Press, 1966), 13.

Mons

Page 150. *"First of all, by what right does a man..."*: Johann Gottlieb Fichte, *Some Lectures Concerning the Scholar's Vocation* (1794), in Paul Franks (trans.), 'The Discovery of the Other: Cavell, Fichte, and Skepticism', *Common Knowledge*, Vol. 5, No. 2, Fall 1996: 86.

Sanctuary Wood

Page 151. *"And the second question..."*: Johann Gottlieb Fichte. *Some Lectures Concerning the Scholar's Vocation* (1794), in Paul Franks (trans.), 'The Discovery of the Other: Cavell, Fichte, and Skepticism', 86. See above note to page 150.

Page 151. *"...as a result of protracted spiritual servitude..."*: Johann Gottlieb Fichte, Preface to "An Attempt at a New Presentation of the Wissenschaftslehre" (1797), in D. Breazeale (trans. and ed.), *J.G. Fichte: Introductions to the Wissenschaftslehre and Other Writings* [1797–1800] (Indianapolis: Hackett, 1994), 5–6. The entire passage, an emotional outburst, reads:

> I wish to have nothing to do with those who, as a result of protracted spiritual solitude, have lost their own selves and, along with this loss of themselves, have lost any feeling for their own conviction, as well as any belief in the conviction of others...I would be sorry if I were understood by people of this sort. To date, this wish has ben fulfilled so far as they are concerned; and I hope that, in the present case as well, these prefatory remarks will so confuse them that from now on, they will be unable to see anything beyond the mere letters, inasmuch as what passes for spirit in their case will be yanked back and forth by the secret fury pent up within them.

Page 152. *"...agreeably relieved of all sense of personal responsibility"*: Siegfried Sassoon, *The Complete Memoirs of George Sherston* (London: Faber and Faber Limited, 1972), 219.

Page 152. *"hidden transformations"*: The term is appropriated from Maurice R. Stein. I took it from John Murray Cuddihy, *The Ordeal of Civility: Freud, Marx, Lévi-Strauss, and the Jewish Struggle with Modernity* (New York: Basic Books, 1974), 14.

Page 153. *"great nature-hater"*: See Ernst Bloch, *The Principle of Hope*, Volume Two, trans. Neville Plaice, Stephen Plaice and Paul Knight. (Cambridge, Massachusetts: The MIT Press, 1995), 549.

Page 153. *"...the ones in whom the seeds of human perfection most decisively lie."*: Johann Gottlieb Fichte, *The Closed Commercial State* (1800), quoted in Ernst Bloch, 554 (see above).

Page 153. *"The question is," said Humpty Dumpty, "which is to be master—that's all."*: Lewis Carroll, *Through the Looking-Glass*, Chapter 6.

Page 154. *"...people of this sort..."*: Johann Gottlieb Fichte, Preface to "An Attempt at a New Presentation of the Wissenschaftslehre" (1797), 5–6. See above note to p. 151.

Saleux

Page 155. *"As if not far from Paradise..."*: Thomas Hardy, "Four in the Morning" in *Human Shows Far Phantasies, Songs and Trifles* (New York: The Macmillan Company, 1925), 31.

Page 157. *"...tears spring to the eyes..."* and *"He himself is destroyed and does not know it"*: from Vincent Monnikendam's startling film, *Mother Dao the Turtlelike* (1996), which re-edits promotional and industrial footage from the Dutch colonial period into a moving elegy for a world which has been destroyed.

Somme

Page 158. *"It is at the edge of the / petal that..."*: William Carlos Williams, *Spring and All* in A. Walton Litz and Christopher MacGowan (eds.), *The Collected Poems of William Carlos Williams: Volume I, 1909–1939* (New York: New Directions, 1986), 195.

Page 159. *"the inexpressible"* and *"This shows itself; it is the mystical."*: Ludwig Wittgenstein, *Tractatus Logico-Philosophicus*, trans. C.K. Ogden (London: Routledge, 1990), 187.

Page 159. *"The sense of the world must lie outside the world."*: Wittgenstein, *Tractatus Logico-Philosophicus*, 183.

Page 160. *"...very disappointed with the reality of the battlefield."*: D.W. Griffith, cited in Paul Virilio, *War and Cinema: The Logistics of Perception*, trans. Patrick Camiller (London: Verso, 1989), 15.

Passchendale

Page 161. *Alfred Hitchcock*. Interview on French TV, cited in Paul Virilio, *War and Cinema: The Logistics of Perception*, trans. Patrick Camiller (London: Verso, 1989), 40.

Bourlon Woods

Page 163. *"One of the largest trees was felled..."*: Stephen A. Spongberg, *A Reunion of Trees: The Discovery of Exotic Plants and Their Introduction into North American and European Landscapes* (Cambridge, Mass.: Harvard University Press ,1990), 135.

Inchy

Page 165. *"Disney says sadly, that Mickey now has to behave."*: "Walt Disney and René Clair (Interviewed)," in *Life and Letters Today*, Vol. XIII, No. 1, September 1935, 199.

Cloven

Page 166. *"clawed their mouths ceaselessly"* and *"Another sucked a rubber tube fastened to the gas-jet."*: Philip Gibbs, *Now It Can Be Told* (New York: Garden City Publishing Co. Ltd., 1920), 550. Gibbs' book is a remarkable indictment of the societies and cultures that encouraged and profited from the First World War, and the only book I know of that publicly exposed, so early, the psychological costs of the war. At least two earlier texts, *Shell Shock and its Lessons*, by G. Elliot Smith and T.H. Pear (Manchester University Press, 1917) and John T. MacCurdy's *War Neuroses* (Cambridge University Press, 1918) were written for the medical profession primarily and take a psychoanalytical approach, urging physicians to recognize neuroses as legitimate, treatable conditions. In his introduction to *War Neuroses*, MacCurdy sums up the situation that faced a shell-shocked soldier in the early years of the war:

Those who had had little sympathy with the neurotic looked on these victims of war as mere malingerers and advised treatment by a firing squad—"pour encourager les autres." Those who had been previously interested in hereditary defects asserted that these new patients were practically all inferior individuals. Those who had emphasized physical factors in peace times were able to demonstrate to their satisfaction that all the cases were suffering from extreme physical fatigue, concussion from high explosive shells, or poisoning with gases from the explosives. On the other hand, there were those who had worked with neurotics from a psychological standpoint, who took the ground that the war neuroses were essentially psychic in origin (3).

MacCurdy discovered that officers were five times more likely to suffer from war neuroses than soldiers. In his introduction, W.H.R. Rivers observes that,

Perhaps the most original feature of [MacCurdy's] work is the view, duly supported by evidence, that those who suffer from anxiety states have wished for death during the period of strain and fatigue preceding the final collapse, while sufferers from conversion hysteria have entertained the desire for disablement, for a "Blighty" wound, or some disabling illness. It is a striking fact that officers are especially prone to the occurrence of anxiety states, while privates are the chief victims of hysterical manifestations. Dr. MacCurdy explains this fact by differences of education and responsibility which produce a different mental outlook towards the two chief means of escape from the rigours and horrors of warfare (vii–viii).

Heir is bot twynklyng of ane e

Page 167. *"Heir is bot twynklyng of ane e"*: William Dunbar, "Full Oft I Mus And Hes In Thocht." Douglas Gray, ed., *Selected Poems of Robert Henryson and William Dunbar* (Harmondsworth: Penguin Books, 1998), 358.

Seed Limit (A Consolation)

Page 168. *Yehuda Amichai (1924–2000)*: Israeli poet. His extraordinary final book, a testament, is *Open Closed Open*, trans. Chana Bloch and Chana Kronfeld (New York: Harcourt Inc., 2000).

Page 168. *Spring and All*: Published in 1923 in Paris in an edition of 300 copies, this text in prose and verse by American poet William Carlos Williams (1883–1963) is a closely-argued poetic manifesto, and Williams' credo. See William Carlos Williams, *Spring and All* in A. Walton Litz and Christopher MacGowan (eds.), *The Collected Poems of William Carlos Williams: Volume I, 1909–1939* (New York: New Directions, 1986).

Page 168. *John Clare (1793–1864)*: English poet and observer of nature and village life who endured, at first hand, the enclosures and the collapse of the old agricultural traditions in Britain. During his final thirty years he spent considerable time in the asylum. He once wrote: "Ah, what a paradise begins with life, and what a wilderness the knowledge of the world discloses! Surely the Garden of Eden was nothing more than our first parents' entrance upon life, and the loss of it their knowledge of the world."

Page 168. *Abraham Moses Klein (1909–1972)*: Montréal poet, author of *The Second Scroll* and *The Rocking Chair*. In 1955 he withdrew from public activity; his final years were spent in silence.

Page 169. *"Thar's the saft seep…"*: Peter Hately Waddell (trans.), The Psalms: frae Hebrew intil Scottis (Edinburgh: Menzies, 1871), 1.

Returning Late

Page 174. *"…grasping one's own mind in its action."*: See Johann Gottlieb Fichte, *Foundations of Natural Right*, ed. Frederick Neuhouser, trans. Michael Baur (Cambridge: Cambridge University Press, 2000), 6.

Page 175. *"Paul Jones of nations"*:.See Herman Melville, *Israel Potter: His Fifty Years of Exile* (New York: Warner Books, Inc., 1974), 159.

The Missions

Page 180. *"This is a song I stole from my sister…"*: Quoted in Claudia Lewis, *Indian Families of the Northwest Coast: The Impact of Change* (Chicago: University of Chicago Press, 1970), 163.

Page 181. *Sussita*: Once a city of 20,000 on the road from Damascus to Scythopolis, and better known by its Greek name, Hippos, this ancient city—founded by the Seleucids in the Early Hellenistic period (332–167 BCE)—sits on a rocky outcrop said to resemble a horse high on the slope of the Golan overlooking the Sea of Galilee, glaring at its traditional foe, the city of Tiberias. Sussita was destroyed by an earthquake in 749 CE, although it has been fought over many times since. Its hillsides are heavily mined and its entrance is still guarded by trenches and bunkers. On the shore of the lake below, Jesus famously exorcised a man beset with devils, transferring them to a hapless herd of pigs which flung themselves into the Sea of Galilee and drowned. See Matthew 8: 28–33, Mark 5: 1–20, Luke 8: 26–39.

Page 182. *Mably*: Quoted in Gordon K. Lewis, *Slavery, Imperialism and Freedom: Essays in English Radical Thought* (London: Monthly Review Press, 1978), 77.

Page 184. *"The value of a uniform in the Services need not be dwelt upon..."*: See John S. Milloy, *A National Crime: The Canadian Government and the Residential School System, 1879 to 1986* (Winnipeg: The University of Manitoba Press, 1999), 125. The text is from the report of the Joint Delegation of Churches to the Minister of Indian Affairs, T.A. Crerar, in November, 1938, taking up the case for school uniforms for aboriginal children in residential schools. Crerar, at one time the President of the United Grain Growers Ltd., was appointed to the federal cabinet in 1917 as Minister of Agriculture in order to placate western farmers hostile to conscription.

Page 185. *"Strange Meadowlark"*: McRae recorded this haunting Brubeck composition on a luminous date with the quartet in New York, December, 1960. *Tonight Only!!! The Dave Brubeck Quartet with Guest Star Carmen McRae* was issued as Columbia recording CL 1609.

Page 185. *"...the old evangelist..."*: Ezra Pound, poet (1885–1972). *"Dorothy..."*: Dorothy Pound (d. 1973), née Shakespear, married Ezra Pound in 1914. For their letters see Omar Pound and Robert Spoo (eds.), *Ezra and Dorothy Pound: Letters in Captivity, 1945–46* (New York: Oxford University Press, 1999), 253 and 270.

Page 185. *"Ou=bee"*: See Ingeborg C.L. Marshall, *Reports and Letters by George Christopher Pulling Relating to the Beothuk Indians of Newfoundland* (St. John's: Breakwater Books, 1989), 26–30 and 141–143.

Page 186. *Mt. Moriah*: Abraham built his altar on Mt. Moriah, which is where he brought Isaac, or Ishmael, at God's command, to be sacrificed. Tradition has it that Mt. Moriah is the today the Haram al-Sharif, or Temple Mount, in Jerusalem.

Page 186. *"The old man..."*: is hiding in a barn in the White Lake basin, between Penticton and Oliver in the Okanagan Valley of British Columbia, a valley alive with meadowlarks and sage thrashers.

ewe

Page 188. *Lady Mary Wortley Montagu (1689–1762)*: A poet and literary figure of her time, best known today for her letters from Constantinople where she lived with her husband, the British ambassador from 1716–1718. In one of these she describes the inoculation parties held each year by old women in Constantinople to protect children against smallpox. Several deep scratches would be made on the limbs of each child and as many drops of smallpox pus as possible would be pushed inside. A nut-shell was tied over the wound to protect it. The recipients would soon take to their beds with a mild case of true smallpox, but within eight days would be recovered. As one who'd been scarred by smallpox herself in 1715, and who had lost a brother to the disease, Lady Mary arranged to have her little son inoculated as soon as possible.

Back in London, she introduced the procedure to several respected British physicians by inoculating her five-year-old daughter in their presence. The process was further tested on eleven charity school children and six inmates of Newgate Prison who volunteered in return for having their death sentences commuted. When all survived, King George I went ahead and had two of his grandchildren inoculated. His example led the way for the acceptance of the procedure.

Page 189. *"Fairest of the young…"* and *"There is no colour,"* etc.: From Lady Mary Wortley Montagu, *Letters from the Right Honourable Lady Mary Wortley Montagu, 1709–1762*, Intro. R. Brimley Johnson (London: J.M. Dent & Co, 1906), 159–160.

Some of these poems have appeared in previous incarnations, in *The Capilano Review*, *Sulphur*, *West Coast Line* and *Writing*. I'm grateful for the support of their editors and guest editors. The photograph of the bronze ewe is by Marian Penner Bancroft. Thank you, Marian, and many thanks also to my dear sisters, Sue and Anna, for providing me with a quiet, secluded room and a big table, and a place to swim on golden evenings.